Authentic Assessment:
A Handbook for Educators

Diane Hart

Addison-Wesley Publishing Company
Menlo Park, California • Reading, Massachusetts
New York • Don Mills, Ontario • Wokingham, England
Amsterdam • Bonn • Sydney • Singapore
Tokyo • Madrid • San Juan • Paris • Seoul
Milan • Mexico City • Taipei

Also in the Assessment Bookshelf:

Open-ended Questioning: A Handbook for Educators
by Robin Lee Harris Freedman

Managing Editor: Michael Kane

Project Editor: Mali Apple

Production Manager: Janet Yearian

Production Coordinator: Claire Flaherty

Design: John F. Kelly

This book is published by Innovative Learning™, an imprint of the
Addison-Wesley Alternative Publishing Group.

ISBN 0-201-81864-7

4 5 6 7 8 9 10 - ML - 97 96 95 94

This Book is Printed
on Recycled Paper

Contents

Introduction

"Mr. James Obechki, age 39, was found lying on the liv-
ing room floor. A chair has been overturned, a broken
lamp is on the floor, and the rug beneath his head has
red stains on it. You will be examining a variety of clues
found at the death site to determine if a crime has been
committed and, if so, which of the several individuals
known to Mr. Obechki could have been present at the site
at the time of his death."[1]

In the spring of 1991, eleventh-grade students across
California were given an array of clues and then asked to use
their scientific training to solve the mystery of Mr. Obechki's
untimely death. Their investigation called on them to apply
skills and knowledge from several branches of science including chemistry (conducting a chromatography test to determine
who wrote a note found on the body), biology (examining hair
samples found at the crime scene with a microscope), and earth
science (analyzing soil samples found on the victim's shoes).

Obviously, this was not your standard machine-scored,
multiple-choice, fill-in-the-bubble science test. The students who
took part in this criminal investigation were field testing a new
approach to science assessment developed for the California
Assessment Program. One objective of this activity was to assess
students' ability to use scientific tools and processes. The activity

would also allow students to demonstrate their understanding of concepts from several fields of science and to communicate their thought processes as they worked toward their conclusions.

Long before the results of the field test were fully analyzed, one thing was clear. Even the most test-jaded students were enthusiastic about this novel approach to assessment. Some liked it so much that they asked to take the test again. One principal reported that students paid the test the ultimate compliment: they talked more about their investigations afterward than about their Friday night parties.

An Assessment Revolution

California's search for alternatives to multiple-choice tests is part of an assessment revolution that is shaking up education from preschools to professional schools. At the heart of this upheaval is the recognition that for all of their virtues—particularly efficiency and economy—traditional standardized tests often fail to tell us what we most want to know about student achievement. Even worse, these same tests exert a powerful and, in the eyes of many educators, pernicious influence on curriculum and instruction by pushing teachers to "teach to the test."

Those at the forefront of the assessment revolution hope to change the way we measure and evaluate what goes on in our schools. In place of standardized tests, they advocate the use of a variety of assessment tools ranging from observation to exhibitions. These alternative means of assessment, they believe, provide a more authentic, or trustworthy, picture of student achievement. Good teachers have long used many of these authentic assessment methods to monitor their own students' progress. What is revolutionary about the new assessment movement is the effort to extend these same methods beyond the classroom to statewide and even national assessment programs.

The assessment revolution began in the late 1980s when a number of states—including California, Rhode Island,

Connecticut, Arizona, Kentucky, Vermont, and New York—
began experimenting with new ways to evaluate student performance. By 1991 at least forty states had plans underway to implement some form of authentic assessment.

Authentic assessment advocates are also having an impact on the effort to create a nationwide examination system in the United States. The purpose of national testing, writes Secretary of Education Lamar Alexander in *America 2000: An Education Strategy,* is "to foster good teaching and learning as well as to monitor student progress." Just how those twin goals are to be realized remains the subject of intense debate. But it is likely that ideas and strategies generated by the authentic assessment movement will find their way into the national testing program.

The purpose of this book

In its brief lifetime, the assessment revolution has spawned a number of exciting approaches to assessment along with a lot of perplexing jargon. The purpose of this book is to help you move beyond the buzzwords toward an understanding of why educators are seeking alternatives to standardized testing and how authentic assessment strategies work.

Where We've Been: Standardized Tests

Mention the words *assessment* and *evaluation* to most people and they think testing. The reason is obvious. For the last half century, most of us have been assessed and evaluated by means of standardized tests. As a result, we tend to think of assessment, evaluation, and testing as interchangeable terms. They are not.

Assessment* is the process of gathering information about students—what they know and can do. There are many ways to gather this information; for example, by observing students as they learn, examining what they produce, or testing their knowledge and skills. The key question in assessment is: How can we find out what students are learning?

Evaluation is the process of interpreting and making judgments about assessment information. By itself assessment data is neither good or bad. It simply mirrors what is going on in the classroom. This information becomes meaningful only when we decide that it reflects something that we value, such as how well a student has mastered long division. The key question in evaluation is: Are students learning what we want them to learn?

Testing is a means of assessment. A ***test*** is simply a measuring instrument used to document student learning. Since the end of World War II, however, testing has dominated assessment and

---

*Boldfaced, italicized terms appear in the assessment glossary at the end of this book.

evaluation. This chapter explores how that domination came about and the reaction to it.

Before Standardized Testing

Testing is an ancient tradition. The Old Testament describes a test devised by Jephthah of Gilead to distinguish between his own men and defeated enemy troops trying to pass as Gileadites in order to escape retribution. Jephthah had his men seize control of a ford on the Jordan River that the defeated troops would have to cross to get home. He then ordered each man who approached the ford to repeat the password "shibboleth," knowing that the enemy troops would be unable to pronounce the "sh" sound properly. Those who failed this early pronunciation test received immediate feedback in the form of on-the-spot executions.[2]

Since the founding of the first schools in colonial times, American students have been asked to demonstrate their learning in structured ways. Horace Mann, the father of public education in the young republic, was a firm believer in testing. As early as 1845 Mann was advocating the use of written tests, with large numbers of questions and standardized answers, to evaluate student performance.

Early research in assessment and evaluation increased interest in standardizing testing. In a study conducted in 1900, copies of a geometry paper were given to 116 teachers for grading. The teachers returned the paper with marks ranging from 28 to 92, a result that raised the obvious questions about their *objectivity,* or freedom from bias and subjectivity.

Equally unsettling results emerged from a later study in which twenty-eight English teachers were given the same paper to grade at two-month intervals. Fifteen of the teachers who initially gave the paper a passing grade failed it the second time. Eleven of the teachers who failed the paper on their first reading gave it a passing grade when they saw it again. Results like these gave strong impetus to a search for more consistent and objective forms of assessment.

The scientific testing movement

The search for more objective assessment tools gave rise to the "scientific testing movement" early in this century. The crowning achievement of this movement was the **standardized test,** a mass-produced multiple-choice test that could be administered to large numbers of people with consistent results. To ensure the accuracy of these tests, the pioneers of scientific testing developed statistical concepts and techniques designed to eliminate such problems as subjectivity in scoring.

By 1928 well over a thousand standardized tests were available in the United States, each with a statistically calculated measure of its **validity** (how well the test measures what it purports to measure) and **reliability** (how constant its scoring results are over time and different test situations). A new age of testing had begun.

The Rise of the Test Industry

The development of standardized tests led to the rise of a new industry. More than a hundred test bureaus were producing standardized tests by the end of World War I. The market for their wares expanded rapidly with the onset of state testing in the 1920s. By 1939 twenty-six states had initiated statewide testing programs.

After World War II, two new trends contributed to the further expansion of the test industry. The first of these was a change in how Americans looked at education. By 1950 the one-room schoolhouse model of individualized instruction had given way to a new model based on the factory and mass production.

The factory model of teaching and testing

The idea that schools could be run as efficient learning factories appealed to Americans in the 1950s. The trick to making the factory-like school work was to break down learning into small skills and bits of knowledge that could be taught and learned sequentially as students moved along the education assembly line.

Standardized tests complemented this model of teaching. With their multiple-choice formats, they were the perfect tool for measuring student mastery of subskills or bits of content. With the advent of computerized scoring, they were inexpensive and easy to use. As a result, standardized tests became the assessment tool of choice for monitoring quality control in the factory school.

The demand for accountability

The second trend that spurred the growth of the test industry was a growing concern about ***accountability.*** During the baby boom years, the amount of money spent on education rose rapidly. But student achievement did not seem to keep pace with this investment. By the 1970s Scholastic Aptitude Test (SAT) scores were falling and employers were complaining that recent high school graduates couldn't read or write. Just what, angry taxpayers began to ask, are we getting for our education dollar? And how can we make teachers and administrators more responsible for the quality of the product that public schools produce?

The answer to both questions seemed to be to measure and to monitor more closely what went on in schools. This meant mandating more testing. Between 1955 and 1986, the amount of money spent on testing students in the United States quadrupled.

In the great push for efficiency and accountability, American education became all but addicted to testing. A 1988 study by the National Center for Fair and Open Testing estimated that United

States public schools administered 105 million standardized test to some 40 million students during the 1986–87 school year. About 55 million tests were mandated achievement, competency, or basic skills tests. The remaining 50 million tests were used in special education programs or for such purposes as screening kindergarten and pre-kindergarten students, identifying gifted and talented students, assessing limited-English-proficient students, and sorting students into different academic tracks.

Types of tests

Regardless of their purpose, most standardized tests fall into two main categories: norm-referenced and criterion-referenced. A **norm-referenced test** is designed to show how a given student or group of students ranks in comparison with other test takers of the same age and grade. The questions on a norm-referenced test are not chosen to reveal what a student knows or can do so much as how that student's performance compares with the performance of his or her peers across the nation. The test scores in newspaper reports comparing student achievement in local schools against a statewide or nationwide norm come from norm-referenced tests.

A **criterion-referenced test** is designed to show how well a student performs relative to an expected standard (what a child should know at a given age) or a specific objective. The items chosen for these tests are intended to reveal a student's strengths and weaknesses in terms of knowledge or skills. **Competency tests** and **achievement tests** are examples of criterion-referenced tests.

While the purposes of these two types of tests differ, both rely on multiple-choice questions. As a result, they look and feel the same to most teachers and students. Of much greater concern to both students and teachers than the type of test is the question of what is riding on the outcome.

When the accountability movement began to take hold, state level people came to realize that they couldn't mandate what teachers were to do in classrooms, but they could mandate a test; and if the test had strong sanctions associated with it, it would modify teachers' behavior.

George Madaus, Director of the Center for the Study of Testing, Evaluation, and Educational Policy[4]

Is the test a ***low-stakes assessment,*** one with few direct
consequences for either students or teachers? Examples of low-
stakes tests include assessments used for diagnostic purposes or
for evaluating curriculum and instruction. In the latter instance,
instructional changes resulting from an assessment may be felt
mainly by students other than those who took the test.

Or is the test a ***high-stakes assessment,*** one in which
something important—a student's promotion, a teacher's evaluation, a school district's certification—hinges on the result?
Because of its importance in college admissions, the SAT is the
ultimate high-stakes test in the eyes of many students. Similarly,
state-mandated reading and math tests that measure and compare student achievement on a classroom, school, and district
basis are viewed as high-stakes tests by most teachers and
administrators. The higher those stakes are seen to be, the more
teachers and administrators are likely to do to make sure that
scores go up.

The Attack on Standardized Tests

Dissatisfaction with standardized tests is as old as the tests
themselves. But as long as the stakes associated with testing were
low, the tests could be dismissed as relatively harmless time
wasters. When the stakes began to rise, the chorus of criticism
grew louder.

Critics raise three main points against standardized tests. The
first is that the tests themselves are flawed. For all the supposed
scientific objectivity of these tests, critics say, the results of standardized testing are often inconsistent, inaccurate, and biased.
These critics also raise doubts about the validity of many tests.
They note that test makers generally validate tests by asking
subject-area specialists to make a judgment as to how well each
test item relates to what the test seeks to measure—a none-too-
scientific method one critic refers to as BOGSAT, an acronym
for Bunch of Guys Sitting Around a Table.

The second criticism raised about standardized tests is that they are a poor measure of anything except a student's test-taking abilities. Those who make this claim point to research showing that for people of similar socioeconomic backgrounds, there seems to be no discernible relationship between standardized test scores and earnings, job competence, scientific or artistic achievements, or other real-life outcomes.

The third point made by these critics is that standardized tests corrupt the very process they are supposed to improve. In their view America's obsession with multiple-choice tests has damaged teaching and learning by

- putting too much value on recall and rote learning at the expense of understanding and reflection.
- promoting the misleading impression that there is a single right answer for most every problem or question.
- turning students into passive learners who need only to recognize, not to construct, answers and solutions.
- forcing teachers to focus more on what can be tested easily than on what is important for students to learn.
- trivializing content and skill development by reducing whatever is taught to a fill-in-the-bubble format.

By the late 1980s, many thoughtful educators had come to the conclusion that for good or ill tests control what goes on in most classrooms, a phenomenon known as WYTIWYG—what you test is what you get. If our goal is to move education away from trivialized or rote learning, they argued, then we will have to change the way we assess students and teachers. And this means looking for alternatives to the machine-scored multiple-choice test.

The corrupting influence of multiple choice has produced a bad bargain between teachers and students: the teachers teach just enough—and in the appropriate form—for students to be able to select the right bubbles. Teachers routinely tell students preparing for the tests: "Don't think! Just mark what you know and move on." But thinking is what everybody needs, including the students.

Ruth Mitchell,
Associate Director
of the Council
for Basic Education[6]

Where We Are Heading: Authentic Assessment

2

The search for alternatives to standardized tests has generated a number of new approaches to assessment under such names as ***alternative assessment, performance assessment, holistic assessment, outcome-based assessment,*** and authentic assessment. While each label suggests slightly different emphases, they all imply a movement toward assessment that supports rather than corrupts exemplary teaching. In this book we have chosen to use ***authentic assessment*** because it emphasizes the development of assessment tools that more accurately mirror and measure what we value in education.

What Makes Assessment Authentic?

An assessment is authentic when it involves students in tasks that are worthwhile, significant, and meaningful. Such assessments look and feel like learning activities, not traditional tests. They involve higher-order thinking skills and the coordination of a broad range of knowledge. They communicate to students what it means to do their work well by making explicit the ***standards*** by which that work will be judged. In this sense authentic assessments are standard-setting, rather than standardized, assessment tools.

Authentic assessments may involve such varied activities as oral interviews, group problem-solving tasks, or the creation of writing portfolios. But in their design, structure, and grading, these new assessment approaches reflect what authentic assessment advocate Grant Wiggins refers to as "criteria of authenticity."[2,3]

Design

In their general design, authentic assessments

- go to the heart of essential learnings, to the understandings and abilities that matter to us.
- are educational and engaging.
- are part of the curriculum rather than arbitrary intrusions with no purpose other than to "shake out a grade."
- reflect real-life, interdisciplinary challenges.
- present students with complex, ambiguous, open-ended problems and tasks that integrate knowledge and skills.
- often culminate in student products or performances.
- are standard setting, pointing students toward higher, richer levels of knowing.
- recognize and value students' multiple abilities, varied learning styles, and diverse backgrounds.

Structure

Authentic assessments are planned and structured so they

- can be attempted by all students, with tasks "scaffolded up" rather than "dumbed down" as necessary.
- are worth practicing for and repeating.
- often require some collaboration with other students.
- are generally known to students in advance, in contrast to traditional **secure,** or secret, tests.
- recognize that different students may need varying amounts of time to complete them.
- may allow for a significant degree of student choice.

Grading

In terms of grading, authentic assessments

- emphasize scoring based on widely shared standards as opposed to easily counted errors.
- reveal and identify students' strengths rather than highlight their weaknesses.
- are scored according to clearly stated performance standards, not a curve or norm.
- assess processes and broad competencies.
- encourage the habit of self-assessment.
- de-emphasize needless and demoralizing comparisons.

The Benefits of Authentic Assessment

Changing the way we assess will inevitably change how teachers teach and how students learn. The advocates of authentic assessment argue that these changes are not only essential to improving education, but will also benefit students, teachers, and families in a number of other ways.

Changing the role of students

Authentic assessment changes the role of students in the assessment process. Instead of being passive test takers, students become active participants in assessment activities—activities that are designed to reveal what they can do instead of highlighting their weaknesses. For students this shift in emphasis often results in decreased test anxiety and increased self-esteem.

Students may benefit from the variety and flexibility of authentic assessment strategies as well. Unlike standardized tests, these assessment tools can be adapted to work well with students of varying abilities, learning styles, and cultural backgrounds.

> It's a common-sense case that says if we value it, we should assess it. . . . If we don't assess it, we won't get it.
>
> **Grant Wiggins**[4]

Finally, authentic assessment presents students with tasks that are interesting, worthwhile, and relevant to their lives. It challenges them to pose questions, make judgments, reconsider problems, and investigate possibilities. It recognizes individual differences and offers choices. For many students, the most important benefit of this approach may be a more positive attitude toward school, learning, and themselves.

Changing the role of teachers

Authentic assessment changes the role of teachers as well as of students. Whereas traditional testing promotes a teacher-centered classroom, authentic assessment requires a more student-centered classroom. In such a classroom, the teacher's main role is to assist students in taking responsibility for their learning and in becoming accomplished self-evaluators.

Teachers who have made the shift to authentic assessments report a number of benefits. Generally, they are more involved in the assessment process, both as designers and evaluators. As a result, they are able to ensure that assessment serves worthwhile curriculum goals. Teachers also find authentic assessments provide them with the information they need both for monitoring student progress and for evaluating their own instructional strategies.

A more active role for parents

The authentic assessment movement also envisions a more active role for parents in assessment. Some schools have already experimented with using parent volunteers as observers and evaluators in some of their new assessments. Parents are being encouraged to look beyond test scores and report cards to evaluate their child's achievement as demonstrated in portfolios and performances.

For many parents, this change is welcome. No longer do they have to master the arcane percentiles and grade equivalencies of standardized test scores to get some idea of how their children are doing. They find that authentic assessments yield clear and concrete information about each child's progress and promise.

Expanding Our Vision of Assessment

The leaders of the authentic assessment movement cheerfully accept the fact that teachers "teach to the test." Schools, they argue, *should* teach to tests—tests that serve our educational goals. And this means expanding our vision of the why, what, and how of assessment.

The why *of assessment*

In the past, educators have recognized three main purposes for assessment:

- *Accountability.* Are we getting value for the money we spend on education?
- *Monitoring.* How well are we doing? As individuals, a class, a school, a district, a state, a nation?
- *Placement.* Which students should be assigned to special programs, promoted, remediated, admitted to college?

To this list, authentic assessment advocates add another purpose:

- *Modeling.* What do we want teachers to teach and how? What do we want students to learn and how?

Looked at this way, assessment becomes a lever for change by providing teachers with concrete models of desirable instruction and student performance. The more an assessment induces changes in instruction to foster the abilities it is designed to assess, the higher its **systemic validity** is said to be.

Beyond school we demonstrate knowledge by providing original conversation and writing, by repairing and building physical objects, and by producing artistic, musical, and athletic performances. In contrast, assessment in school usually asks students to identify the discourse, things, and performances that others have produced.

Doug Archibald,
Center for Policy
Research in Education
Fred Newmann,
Center on Effective
Secondary Schools[6]

The what *of assessment*

For years, both teachers and test developers were guided by the motto: "If it can't be tested, it isn't worth teaching." The result was an overemphasis on the teaching of easily tested skills and content knowledge.

The authentic assessment movement turns this motto around by saying, "If it's worth learning, it's worth assessing." If we want students to write well, we should assess their writing. If we want students to learn how to solve problems using mathematical knowledge, our assessments should give them such problems to solve. If we want students to analyze, interpret, synthesize, and evaluate information, we must assess those skills in a meaningful context.

This does not mean giving up the assessment of content knowledge. In authentic assessment, knowledge and skills are essential and inseparable. In authentic assessment tasks, however, content knowledge becomes a means to an end, not the end in itself.

The how *of assessment*

When most people think about how to assess students, they think of testing. In authentic assessment, however, tests are just one of many modes of assessment. These different assessment modes are often grouped into three broad categories based on the kind of information they provide about students:

- *observations,* or information gathered mainly by teachers in their daily work with students.
- *performance samples,* or tangible products that serve as evidence of student achievement.
- *tests* and test-like procedures, or measures of student achievement at a particular time and place.

In the next three chapters, we will take a closer look at each of these assessment categories.

We can assess students in a variety of ways: we can observe what they do, listen to what they say, read what they write, and analyze what they produce. Any behavior that can be perceived can be adapted for assessment.

George Hein,
Professor of Liberal Studies and Adult Learning Programs, Lesley College[7]

Observing What Students Do

3

Meela flops down on a pile of cushions with her reading teacher and picks up a book to read aloud. As Meela reads, her teacher watches and listens carefully, noting specific reading behaviors on a typed transcript of the book. Afterward, Meela talks about the story she has just read with her teacher, who jots down notes on a simple form. Before Meela leaves, the teacher shares some observations with her, pointing out, for example, how Meela figured out an unfamiliar word. Later the teacher uses her observations and notes to evaluate Meela's reading patterns and to select strategies that should help Meela improve in the months ahead.

Observation is probably our oldest means of assessment. From the time of Socrates onward, good teachers have monitored their students to assess their progress. They have also adjusted their instructional approach based on what they see and hear. With the rise of standardized tests, however, observation was largely ignored as a formal means of assessment.

Observation is once again becoming a valued assessment tool. No other form of assessment, its advocates claim, yields as rich and coherent a picture of each student's development. Meela's reading teacher would probably agree with this assertion. By observing Meela read, she has learned far more about this student's strengths, weaknesses, interests, and attitudes as a reader than any test would have revealed.

Observation-based Assessment

A teacher wanders around the classroom with clipboard in hand and periodically makes a note about a student. This is the essence of observation. To make observation an accepted and effective assessment tool, however, three issues need to be addressed. How do we make observation a systematic part of an assessment program? How do we focus observation on what we most want to know about students? And how do we document observations without overwhelming ourselves with paperwork?

Making observation systematic

Teacher observations are by their nature informal and anecdotal. Even so, observation can be made a more systematic part of an assessment program by following a few simple guidelines:

- Observe all students.
- Observe often and regularly.
- Record observations in writing.
- Note the typical as well as the atypical. Observations of the routine are just as valuable as observations of the extraordinary.
- Aggregate multiple observations to enhance their reliability. One instance does not a pattern make.
- Synthesize evidence from different contexts to increase the validity of observations.

What to look for

Knowing what to look for is also important to observation-based assessment. An inexperienced observer listening to Meela read would probably hear only her mistakes. A knowledgeable observer would hear how Meela deals with unfamiliar words and constructs meaning while she reads. Similarly, a parent looking at a young child's first attempts at writing might see only scribbles. Looking at those same scribbles, an experienced teacher would see an emergent writer who has begun to develop important concepts about print.

One of the most widely used tools for helping observers focus on what to look for is the ***developmental checklist.*** Such a checklist describes the ***traits,*** or learning behaviors, the observer should be assessing. When used repeatedly over the school year, developmental checklists provide a clear picture of student progress over time.

Developmental checklists can be adapted to almost any observation purpose. In the primary grades, they are generally used to focus attention on specific learning behaviors such as the use of punctuation in writing. In early childhood education programs, many teachers use developmental checklists to help them track their students' progress through predictable stages of development. An example of a developmental checklist used to assess the development of block-building skills in young children is shown on page 18.

Another useful tool for focusing observation is the ***interview sheet,*** also known as the conference recording form. Interview sheets take many forms, depending on what the interviewer hopes to observe. Generally they consist of a list of questions the teacher plans to ask students and space for recording the responses. The interview sheet on page 19 is used in whole language programs to gain insight into how students feel about the stories they have read.

Documenting what is observed

For observations to be considered credible, they must be documented. And recording information takes time. The most common concern teachers raise about observation-based assessment is that it will be too time-consuming. This is especially true for teachers with large classes. Without some outside assistance from aides or volunteers, many teachers find it nearly impossible to

Developmental Stages in Block Building[2]

Stage 1 Blocks are carried around, not used for construction.

Stage 2 Building begins. Children make mostly rows, either horizontal (on the floor) or vertical (stacking). There is much repetition in this early building pattern.

Stage 3 Bridging: two blocks with a space between them, connected by third block.

Stage 4 Enclosures: blocks placed in such a way that they enclose a space.

Stage 5 When facility with blocks is acquired, decorative patterns appear. Much symmetry can be observed. Buildings, generally, are not yet named.

Stage 6 Naming of structures for dramatic play begins. Before that, children may also have named their structures, but the names were not necessarily related to the function of the building.

Stage 7 Children's buildings often reproduce or symbolize actual structures they know, and there is a strong impulse toward dramatic play around the block structures.

focus their attention on observing one child at a time. Nor do they have time for extensive record keeping.

Many teachers, however, have found ways to keep the time burden of observation manageable. The key is to create a system of note taking and record keeping that minimizes writing and recording time.

At the center of most record-keeping systems is a loose-leaf notebook, a file box, or a computerized database with a section or file for each student. This is where notes and observations about students are collected and organized throughout the school year.

Some teachers use a simple class form for recording anecdotal information about students each week. Typically this form has the names of students running down the left side and the days of the

Literature Interview Sheet[3]

Reader's Name_____ Date _____

Interviewer's Name _____

Book Title_____

Author _____

1. Whom did you like most in the story?

2. Whom did you like least?

3. Where does the story take place?

4. When does the story take place?

5. Why did the story keep your interest?

6. Did the author do anything that surprised you?

7. What was the saddest part of the story?

8. What was the happiest part of the story?

9. Did any part of the story make you laugh or cry?

10. What do you wish you could ask the author?

11. What do you think you will remember about this book?

12. What type of person do you think would most enjoy reading this book?

week across the top. At the end of each week, the notes on this form are transferred to each student's individual record.

To minimize note transfer time, many teachers record their anecdotal observations on self-stick address labels. Later these labels can be affixed to student records without recopying. Some teachers even preprint pages of labels with their students' names. This not only saves time when making notes, but also lets them know at a glance which students have and have not been observed recently.

Well-designed developmental checklists and interview sheets also help teachers capture useful information efficiently. The checklists below and on page 21 make tracking student development a simple matter of noting dates.

While many teachers create their own record-keeping systems, some schools are beginning to experiment with more formalized observation-based assessment and documentation systems. One such system is the Primary Language Record, which was developed in Great Britain in the 1980s and is now being tested in New York, New Jersey, and California schools.

Group Developmental Record Sheet [5]									
SYMBOLIC DEVELOPMENT IN ART									
✎	✎	O	☺	☼	🧍	🏠	🏠	🏠	🏠
Alicia 8/29	9/1	11/2							
Hoa			8/29						
Carol			8/29	9/16					
David			9/15						

Individual Record of Developmental Milestones

Name _Gilberto_

SYMBOLIC PLAY RECORD				
Stage 1	*Stage 2*	*Stage 3*	*Stage 4*	*Stage 5*
Real object	Similar object	Dissimilar object	No object	Sociodramatic play
8/29	9/15			

INVENTED SPELLING STAGES				
Stage 1	*Stage 2*	*Stage 3*	*Stage 4*	*Stage 5*
Initial consonant	Initial, final consonants	Initial, medial, final consonants	Vowel as place holder	Standard spelling
9/15	11/2			

The Primary Language Record consists of two four-page forms that together create a complete record of each child's language arts development during the school year. The first form, "Observations and Samples," is used to collect data about a student's reading experiences, writing activities, and use of oral language on a regular basis. The first page of this form is reproduced on page 22.

This observation data is periodically summarized by teachers on a second form, the "Primary Language Record." These summaries are supplemented by observations from other staff members and information gleaned from teacher conferences with parents and students. The form concludes with a section of information and recommendations for the teacher who will receive the student the following year.

The Primary Language Record has been successful as an assessment tool because it provides a well-documented and rich picture of a student's progress in language arts. Also, it improves teaching. As a head teacher in Britain observed, "It really stops the teachers talking so much and makes them listen."[7]

> I used to teach children and evaluate their progress. But now I kid watch, facilitate the learning of children, and try to discover why learners do what they do. I have learned to celebrate children's strengths as language users.
>
> *Anonymous Teacher* [6]

The Primary Language Record

Name _____ Year Group _____

1 *Talking and listening: diary of observations*

The diary below is for recording examples of the child's developing use of talk for learning and for interacting with others in English and/or other community languages.

Include different kinds of talk (e.g. planning an event, solving a problem, expressing a point of view or feelings, reporting on the results of an investigation, telling a story).

Note the child's experience and confidence in handling social dimensions of talk (e.g. initiating a discussion, listening to another contribution, qualifying former ideas, encouraging others).

The matrix sets out some possible contexts for observing talk and listening. Observations made in the diary can be plotted on the matrix to record the range of social and curriculum contexts sampled.

	SOCIAL CONTEXTS				
LEARNING CONTEXTS	pair	small group	child with adult	small/large group with adult	
collaborative reading and writing activities					
play, dramatic play, drama, and storying					
environmental studies and historical research					
math and science investigations					
design, construction, craft, and art projects					

Dates	Observations and their contexts

Evaluating Students' Work: Portfolio Assessment

4

Scott, a fourth grader in an inner-city school, unpacks a folder of his work while explaining to his resource teacher the significance of each item. He pulls out a drawing ("This shows that I can draw pictures, because before I couldn't draw."), a written piece ("Before I couldn't write that good, and now I can."), a list of books he has read ("This says that I'm a reader, that I can read these books."), and his report card from third grade ("This is the best report card I ever had."). While Scott may not test well, the body of work in his folder reveals a student who has made significant strides in a year. Scott's reflections on his work show that he is aware of and feels good about his progress.[1]

Scott and his resource teacher are participants in a growing movement to assess students' progress by evaluating tangible examples of their work. There are many ways to collect and organize student work for assessment, such as writing folders and science notebooks. The approach that has generated the most interest, however, is one borrowed from artists and designers: the creation of a portfolio to show the range and quality of an individual's work.

Portfolio Assessment

A **portfolio** is a container that holds evidence of an individual's skills, ideas, interests, and accomplishments. It can be as basic as a folder stuffed with selected papers, as fancy as a decorated notebook showcasing polished writing samples, or as high tech as a laser disk with stored images of a student's accomplishments. Whatever form a portfolio takes, it should be more than a collection of stuff. A well-designed portfolio contains a thoughtfully organized body of work.

Unlike a test, which provides a snapshot of student achievement at a particular time and place, a portfolio documents learning over time. It is this long-term perspective that makes portfolios such a useful assessment tool. Looked at individually, a portfolio can reveal how well a student is progressing in a given skill or subject. Looked at collectively, a group of portfolios can be used to evaluate curriculum and instruction within a classroom, across a school district, or throughout an entire state.

Portfolio assessment may prove to be particularly appropriate for culturally disadvantaged and limited-English-proficient students. These students often dread traditional testing, knowing that they will score poorly. With portfolio assessment, the emphasis is on what students can do, not on their deficiencies relative to some norm. The positive feedback culturally disadvantaged students receive when they share their portfolios with teachers, family members, and peers can transform assessment from a demoralizing to an affirming experience. This was true for the junior high school student who wrote of his first portfolio assessment:

> *"I thought nobody liked me, and nobody wanted to be with me. But after I put my portfolio together, I found people do like me and want me to be around them. They want me to do good. . . ."*[3]

Purpose of portfolios

A well-designed assessment portfolio can serve four distinct purposes. It can enable

- teachers to assess student growth and progress.

- parents and teachers to communicate more effectively about a student's work.
- teachers and supervisors to evaluate instructional programs.
- students to become partners with teachers in the assessment process.

For many teachers this last purpose is particularly important. The simple process of assembling a portfolio requires making judgments about what work to include and why. To do this students must apply evaluation standards to their own efforts. And as they do so, they begin to develop the habit of self-assessment. "The greatest asset of portfolios, I've found, is in self-evaluation," writes Darlene M. Frazier, a teacher at West Orient School in Gresham, Oregon. "Portfolio assessment offers students a way to take charge of their learning; it also encourages ownership, pride, and high self-esteem."[5]

I'm breathing a sigh of relief that we are finally coming around to documenting and evaluating the growth that I just know is happening in my classroom.

Mary Jo Kever,
Fourth-grade Teacher,
Holy Trinity School,
Des Moines, Iowa[4]

Contents of portfolios

One of the first questions that arises when considering portfolio assessment is what should go into a portfolio. As the figure below suggests, the possibilities seem almost endless.

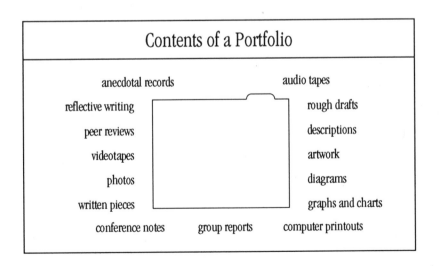

Contents of a Portfolio

anecdotal records   audio tapes
reflective writing   rough drafts
peer reviews   descriptions
videotapes   artwork
photos   diagrams
written pieces   graphs and charts
conference notes   group reports   computer printouts

What goes into a portfolio depends on its purpose. Is it to be used mainly for encouraging self-assessment? For a teacher's assessment of individual students? For broader assessment purposes? Contents will also vary with intended audience. Who will be looking at the portfolio? Students? Families? Teachers? Administrators? Possible employers? Finally, what is included will reflect what the audience most wants to see. A student's very best work? A record of process from first drafts to final product? Evidence of growth and change over time?

Thoughtfully selected examples of student work form the core of most portfolios. Work samples, however, tell only part of the story. Students' reflections on their work are also important. For this reason most portfolios include self-evaluations and reflective statements. This is what eighth-grader Justin Brown wrote about his growth as a poet after reflecting on the work in his portfolio:

> *My poems were very basic in the beginning; they were all rhymed haiku because that was all I knew about. Then I experimented with going with the feelings or ideas . . . don't kill yourself going over the rhymes, go with what you feel. I did that for two months. Then I started compacting them, shortening them to make deeper meaning. I could see that it would make more of a point if I washed out the the's and and's and if's. Now I am working on something different. . . . I am not trying to write how I feel only, but metaphors.*[7]

Evaluating portfolios

How portfolios are evaluated depends on their purpose. In classrooms where one of the main goals of creating portfolios is to encourage the habit of self-assessment, teachers often ask students to establish their own evaluation criteria. "It's got to come from them and their language," says Sally Loughlin, a third-grade teacher at Narragansett School in Gorham, Maine. In the view of Loughlin's students, writing is "great" when it is original, uses varied sentence structures, shows consideration for the reader, and is work the author feels proud to have written.[8]

When the purpose is to measure and track student growth, there is some debate about how this should be done using portfolios. On one side are those who believe that setting school- or districtwide standards for assessing portfolios smacks of standardization and will lead to lumping students into categories again. Those who hold this view argue that teachers should be left alone to evaluate portfolios according to their own standards or grading systems. On the other side of this debate are those who believe standards are needed, if only to assure some continuity and accountability in assessment. The standards applied to portfolio assessment, they argue, should be developed within the framework of both local and state expectations for students.

When portfolios are used to evaluate instructional programs on a district- or statewide basis, assessment standards are clearly essential. So is some means of **sampling,** or selecting a subset of portfolios to represent the entire student population. In a pilot study of portfolio-based writing assessment carried out in Durham, New Hampshire, researchers evaluated the district's fifth-grade writing program by analyzing a randomly selected sample of twenty-seven student portfolios. The time and expense involved in this effort compared favorably to the cost of assessing all fifth graders with a timed writing test. The portfolio assessment, however, yielded more detailed information about student writers than the writing test. It also indicated that the timed test underrated the writing ability of many students.[10]

Using the results

In many schools portfolios are being used to supplement traditional methods of reporting student progress, especially to parents. Crow Island School in Winnetka, Illinois, holds a series of "Portfolio Evenings" each year during which small groups of

> Portfolios allow me to assess writing without grading everything students write. That is, I assess only those pieces which students confer about, revise, and edit thoroughly rather than all the pieces they have written.
>
> **Margie Krest,**
> *English Teacher,*
> *Thornton High School,*
> *Thornton, Colorado*[9]

students meet with their parents to present their portfolios. While the teacher is there to add comments, the students are expected to "run the show"—and they do. Both parents and teachers have been impressed by the leadership and independence shown by even very young students during their portfolio presentations.[11]

Sand Creek Elementary School in Colorado took portfolio assessment a step further when it abandoned report cards and parent-teacher conferences in favor of portfolio "progress reports" and parent-teacher-student conferences. A survey of parents on the new assessment system revealed that about two-thirds thought the new progress reports gave them a clear picture of their child's achievements. Even so, they missed letter grades. As a result, report cards were added back the following year. "It's pretty clear that parents want a combination of both," concluded Sand Creek principal Gary Poole.[13]

Vermont is using information gained from portfolio assessment to evaluate and improve writing and mathematics programs across the state. In one school, for example, teachers discovered a significant lack of poetry samples when they evaluated their students' portfolios according to state standards. The reason was that most of them covered poetry only once, at the end of the year. "Portfolio assessment helped me refocus," reported one teacher. "It made me realize that I need to do poetry more than once a year."[14]

A Portfolio Sampler

Interest in portfolio assessment has blossomed at every level of education in the past few years. At first limited to arts and language arts classes, portfolios are used today in math, science, and social science classrooms as well. A few schools are finding even more unusual applications. Here, then, is a sampler of five quite different uses of portfolios in assessment.

Algebra portfolios

In 1991 Pam Knight, a math teacher at Twin Peaks Middle School in Poway, California, decided to experiment with portfolios in her algebra class. Not knowing quite what to expect from her students, she was not certain at first whether portfolios would work with math. When she saw what her students put together, however, Knight decided to make portfolio assessment a permanent part of her math program.[15]

Purposes

- To encourage student self-assessment
- To supplement traditional means of grading
- To provide information for evaluating the instructional program

Contents

- Five items selected by students to represent their math knowledge and effort
- Table of contents
- Personal statement explaining why each piece was important

  One student's reflection began:

  I chose these papers for my portfolio because they show my best work and my worst work. They portray both sides of my academic performance in math this semester.

Evaluation

Knight had students grade each other's portfolios using a grading sheet she provided and then added her own comments. She reports that students not only benefited from the immediate feedback, but also found it helpful to see what others had done in their portfolios.

My students are now collecting work for their next try, which they are calling "Son of Portfolio." ... Math portfolios are a wonderful way for students to celebrate their learning.

Pam Knight,
Math Teacher,
Twin Peaks Middle School,
Poway, California[16]

Uses

Knight made portfolio grades one component of semester grades. She also reports using what she learned from her students' portfolios to reevaluate her curriculum:

> *It became apparent early on that if I wanted variety in my children's portfolios, I had to provide variety in assignments. I have changed my curriculum to include more problem-solving opportunities with written explanations. I have also had my students do two long-term situational problems. In the past, although I knew my algebra classes found such projects entertaining, I had questioned their lasting value. Now I see that these problems are the ones the kids remember most.*

Employability skills portfolios

Michigan has put portfolios at the center of a statewide effort to prepare students for the workplace. In 1990 Michigan piloted a program that will eventually have every student create a personal Employability Skills Portfolio. The pilot study involved more than five thousand students from grades six through twelve in regular, special, and vocational education. Each school involved in the pilot study developed its own approach toward implementing the portfolio process.[17]

Purposes

- To enable students to discover, develop, strengthen, and document their employability skills
- To help all students gain the skills and confidence they need to succeed in employment whether they plan to work while in school, after graduation, or after college
- To provide data for program evaluation

Contents

- Information guide for students and teachers
- Profile of the key employability skills (see page 31)

Employability Skills Profile

ACADEMIC SKILLS

- Read and understand written materials
- Understand charts and graphs
- Understand basic math
- Use mathematics to solve problems
- Use research and library skills
- Use specialized knowledge and skills to get a job done
- Use tools and equipment
- Speak in the language in which business is conducted
- Write in the language in which business is conducted
- Use scientific method to solve problems

PERSONAL MANAGEMENT SKILLS

- Attend school/work daily and on time
- Meet school/work deadlines
- Develop career plans
- Know personal strengths and weaknesses
- Demonstrate self-control
- Pay attention to details
- Follow written and oral instructions
- Follow written and oral directions
- Work without supervision
- Learn new skills
- Identify and suggest new ways to get the job done

TEAMWORK SKILLS

- Actively participate in a group
- Know the group's rules and values
- Listen to other group members
- Express ideas to other group members
- Be sensitive to the group members' ideas and views
- Be willing to compromise if necessary to best accomplish the goal
- Be a leader or a follower to best accomplish the goal
- Work in changing settings and with people of differing backgrounds

- Evidence of student's attainment of employability skills in academics, personal management, and teamwork. Such evidence might include sample schoolwork, transcripts, achievement test scores, personal honors and awards, journals, letters from teachers and employers, a résumé, a personal career plan, documentation of team or group membership, news articles, and photographs or videotapes of completed projects.
- Guide designed to encourage parental participation in the portfolio process
- Summary sheet of skills for use in preparing for job interviews

Evaluation

Evaluation varies from school to school. One promising approach is to have local business representatives review portfolios and provide students with feedback on their strengths and weaknesses along with tips for improving their skills and documentation.

Uses

Project organizers are working to create a meaningful scoring system for evaluating Employability Skills Portfolios on a broad scale. Their goal is to provide useful feedback to local districts and the state for program evaluation and improvement.

Arts PROPEL writing portfolios

Arts PROPEL is a five-year cooperative project based on the research conducted at Harvard Project Zero, which argues that artistic ability is a form of intelligence that should be nurtured by schools along with other intelligences. The project brought artists, educators from Harvard Project Zero, and researchers from the Educational Testing Service into the Pittsburgh public schools with the goal of transforming arts education from a "frill" into an essential part of the curriculum. The program that emerged from this collaboration focuses on three areas: music, the visual arts, and creative writing. Students are taught to develop their skills in these areas through a three-stage creative process involving production, perception, and reflection (for which PROPEL is a loose acronym). Student portfolios are an important part of Arts PROPEL classes.[18]

Purposes

- To provide evidence of growth and change
- To encourage reflection and self-assessment
- To document the creative process from inception to final product
- To document the range of work a student has produced over time
- To establish a "portfolio culture" in Arts PROPEL classrooms

Contents

While there are no standard portfolios in the Arts PROPEL program, a writing portfolio might include some or all of the following items:

- Writing inventory discussing the student's experience as a writer
- Biography of a work that illustrates the entire writing process from first draft to final product (see page 34)
- An important piece of writing along with the student's reasons for its selection and reflections on the experience of writing this piece
- A satisfying piece and an unsatisfying piece with a discussion of the qualities that led to their selection
- Student's free pick with reasons for this choice
- Optional teacher-student negotiated pick if another piece is needed to document the range of a student's work
- Final reflections about the pieces chosen for the portfolio and about the student's growth as a writer

Portfolios are messy. They demand intimate and often frighteningly subjective talk with students. Portfolios are work. Teachers who ask students to read their own progress in the "footprints" of their works have to coax and bicker with individuals who are used to being assessed. Halfway through the semester, at least half a dozen recalcitrants will lose every paper or sketch or tape they have ever owned.

Dennie Palmer Wolf,
Research Associate, Project
Zero, Harvard Graduate
School of Education [19]

Drafts of a Poem from an Arts PROPEL Portfolio

First Draft	Second Draft	Third Draft
the goose strutted on the shore, in the dried out grass and the sun bleached straw as if ~~like~~ it blew the reasons why the ducklings splashed in the ~~sat~~ water by the road, and why the truck ~~that cause~~ that rambled it's way ~~on~~ along the highway stopped to gaze at the ~~stillness that was~~ broken broken only by ~~somedy~~ the splash of water against more water and the repeated flap of the gooses' webbed feet against ~~the soft prairie grass and~~ ~~the goose strutted on the shore~~ ~~in the dried out the grass~~ the shore	2/ the goose strutted on the shore in the dried out grass and the sun bleached straw as if it knew the reasons why the ducklings spla~~#~~shed in the water ~~be~~ by the road, and why the truck that at first rambled it's way along the highway stopped to gaze in appreciation with ~~first~~ just total and just remembered memories mixed ~~of~~ in the broken stillness, broken only by the splash of water against more water, and the repeated flap of the gooses' webbed feet against the ~~padded grasses and~~ soft earth.	3/ the goose strutted on the shore, In the dried out grass And the sun bleached straw As if it knew The reasons why the ducklings splashed in the water by the road, And why the truck, That at first rambled it's way Along the highway Stopped to gaze in appreciation with just remembered memories Mixed in the broken stillness, Broken only by the splish Of water against more water, and the repeated Flap of the gooses' webbed feet against the soft earth.

34 *Authentic Assessment*

Evaluation

Criteria for evaluation of PROPEL portfolios vary according to the type and purpose of the portfolio. PROPEL teachers, however, have worked to put students at the center of the assessment process by

- providing writing opportunities in new genres.
- having students examine other authors' work.
- encouraging collaboration with peers.
- asking students to share their work with others.
- having students critique their own work.
- encouraging revision of work.

Uses

While students use portfolios to document their growth, Arts PROPEL teachers are using those same portfolios to assess their teaching methods and skills. Once a year teachers select three to five portfolios illustrating exceptional, moderate, or limited progress in writing to share with their supervisor. Teacher and supervisor then meet to "do portfolios." During these discussions teachers use student portfolios to illustrate their instructional program and to highlight particular problems or points of progress. "PROPEL has changed my teaching tremendously," reports teacher Linda Ross-Broadus. "Before . . . I did most of the talking. Now the students are taking charge of their work."[20]

Laser disk portfolios

Teachers and students at Conestoga Elementary School in rural Wyoming are working with IBM and researchers from Harvard Project Zero to explore the use of multimedia technology to create portfolios on laser disks. The laser disk has obvious virtues as a portfolio storage medium. It can be used to record anything from scanned images of a student's written work to videotapes of a student reading aloud, playing a game, or throwing a pot. Large amounts of data can be added to and retrieved from a disk quite easily. Yet the disk itself is small enough to slip into a child's permanent file with no need for additional storage space.[21]

Purposes

- To provide a continuous record of each student's growth in verbal ability, artistic achievement, physical accomplishments, and self-assurance
- To facilitate individualizing of instruction to fit the needs and interests of each child
- To build self-esteem by having students' achievements recorded and measured against individual standards, not group norms

Contents

Because this is a cumulative portfolio, the contents expand year by year. The contents also vary depending on what each teacher chooses to add and what students themselves elect to include in their portfolios. Some of those records might include

- preassessment videos made early in the year of students reading aloud, playing a game, or answering questions
- samples of student writing
- images of student drawings and artwork
- videos documenting a new skill such as tying one's shoes or throwing a basketball through the hoop
- videos of special projects or performances

Evaluation

Criteria for evaluating student growth have been developed by grade-level teacher teams. Formal assessment takes place twice a year, and more often if needed, when teachers meet with students to review their portfolios and discuss their progress.

Uses

Conestoga is using laser disk portfolios as part of its permanent record for each student. The school also plans to make portfolios the centerpiece of an annual ritual of passage for students

Portfolio assessment is not a new concept in education, but a system that allows permanent storage of optical data, written and drawn images, and verbal ability *is* new.

Jo Campbell,
Principal, Conestoga
Elementary School,
Gillette, Wyoming[22]

graduating from sixth grade. During this ritual each student will meet with his or her parents, teacher, and principal to review the student's portfolio from kindergarten to graduation.

"We are expecting tears and laughter and possibly embarrassment from students viewing their antics of years gone by," writes principal Jo Campbell, "but we are also predicting that every family will want a copy of the disk for a personal history."

Teaching portfolios

In many schools of education today, student teachers are encouraged or required to create teaching portfolios as part of their training process. Teaching portfolios are also being used by experienced teachers to document and communicate their teaching styles, skills, and philosophy.

Purposes

- To provide information for evaluation and self-assessment
- To document teaching activities for students, parents, peers, and supervisors
- To provide concrete examples for presentations and in-service training

Contents

A teaching portfolio might contain any of the following and more:

- Description of the teaching setting—community, school, students, colleagues, and so on
- Videotape of teaching
- Evaluations from students, peers, and supervisors
- Self-appraisal of teaching skills and description of steps taken to improve performance, such as attending workshops and classes
- List of professional affiliations, publications, and activities
- Sample lesson plans, student handouts, homework assignments, and other teaching tools

- Samples or videotapes of student projects and performances
- Reflections on one's goals and growth as a teacher

Evaluation

Evaluation criteria for assessing teaching portfolios vary from school to school and teacher to teacher. The most important evaluations may be those teachers make themselves about their effectiveness in the classroom.

Uses

Teaching portfolios are already an important assessment tool in teacher education programs. In the future, portfolios may become part of the teacher certification and licensure process in some states. Many teachers find teaching portfolios useful in documenting and communicating their teaching methods. In presentations to other teachers, Ron Berger, a sixth-grade teacher at Schutesbury Elementary School in Massachusetts, uses a portfolio of his students' work to illustrate his "project workshop" approach to teaching. "When I start to feel that my descriptions of this approach to learning are mostly hot air, a hype, another new gimmick in the age-old and rarely improved business of teaching," he writes, "I have something real and tangible to renew my faith, to share with others." Berger adds that:

> *These projects and the accomplishments they represent for students are evidence for me that many aspects of the "good old days" can be substantially improved upon. . . . Almost nothing I created during 13 years of schooling was an artifact that I treasured, that I kept and admired over the years. In contrast, the work I carry around today is on loan from students. Many students were unwilling to part with their projects, even for a year, so I could use them in workshops; those who agreed were sometimes nervous about it.*[23]

Testing What We Care About: Performance Assessment

5

A few years ago, high school math teacher Bill Hadley took time out to do "a thorough self-evaluation of my own assessment practices." He reached the following conclusions:

> *First, I found that the only reason for some of my tests was to produce a number to put in my rollbook. I was receiving very little information about my students' learning or abilities from these exams. Second, it became more and more apparent to me that as I was constructing my tests, I was able to accurately predict which of my students would be able to answer individual questions. Finally, I realized that unless I designed tests that would provide opportunities for students who worked at different paces to demonstrate their abilities, I was testing speed rather than learning. . . .*

The following year, Hadley decided to use **performance tasks** rather than traditional tests to evaluate students in his general math class.

> *I assigned groups or pairs of students certain tasks to perform. Then by coaching, observing, and interviewing the students as they worked on these tasks, I was able to assess their knowledge and growth. The information I received was much more comprehensive and complete, and I found that I was able to give the students grades*

that I thought very accurately reflected their progress. The students for the most part agreed.[1]

Bill Hadley is one of many teachers who are experimenting with new kinds of tests and test-like procedures to assess their students. In this chapter we will look at a new approach to testing known as **performance assessment**. Unlike traditional tests that focus on facts and discrete skills, performance assessments are designed to test what we care about most—the ability of students to use their knowledge and skills in a variety of realistic situations and contexts.

Performance Assessment

There is nothing fundamentally new about performance assessment. For centuries, master artisans have assessed their apprentices by observing how they perform specific tasks. Music maestros have assessed their students by listening to them perform. Coaches have assessed athletes by watching their performances in games and meets. In all three the performance being assessed is authentic in that it reflects the real demands of the craft, art, or sport.

Performance assessment tries to bring this same sense of authenticity to the classroom by presenting students with tasks that simulate real-world challenges and problems. In such tasks there is seldom one right way to approach the problem or one correct response. Performance tasks are active assessments. Often they are done by students working collaboratively. Above all, writes Grant Wiggins, such tasks are "enticing, feasible, and defensible—tests worth taking."[3]

Performance assessment goals

Performance tasks can be used to assess a wide variety of learning outcomes. They are particularly useful, however, for assessing understandings, complex skills, and habits of thought that are not usually addressed by conventional tests. A growing concern that students develop such competencies has led a number of states to incorporate performance assessment into their statewide testing plans.

One of the leaders in this effort is Kentucky, which has made performance assessment an integral part of its educational reform program. Kentucky is developing performance tasks to test students' progress toward six broad goals:

- applying basic communication and mathematics skills
- applying core concepts and principles from all subject matter disciplines
- becoming a self-sufficient individual
- becoming a productive member of a family, work group, or community
- thinking and problem solving
- connecting and integrating knowledge

The performance task entitled Documenting Biological Succession (see page 55) illustrates how several of these goals can be addressed in a single activity.[5]

Performance tasks

Performance tasks are as varied as the goals they serve. They may be short test-like tasks created to assess relatively specific knowledge and skills. Or they may be lengthy, complex tasks designed to assess broad knowledge, processes, and competencies. Such tasks may be more or less "authentic" insofar as they simulate real-life situations and problems.

Designing performance tasks is a challenge. Good tasks grow out of the curriculum. They are feasible in terms of available time and resources. They are inviting to both teachers and students. And the results can be scored and reported in ways that satisfy students, teachers, parents, administrators, as well as district or state testing directors. Grant Wiggins suggests the following

In today's political climate, tests are inadequate and misleading as measures of achievement. Assessment tasks should be redesigned—indeed, are being redesigned—to more closely resemble real learning tasks.

Lorrie A. Shepard,
Professor of Education,
University of Colorado
at Boulder[4]

questions should be addressed in the design of performance assessments.[6]

- What kinds of essential tasks, achievements, habits of mind, or other valued "masteries" are falling through the cracks of conventional tests?
- What are the core performances, roles, or situations that all students should encounter and be expected to master?
- What are the most salient and insightful discriminators in judging actual performances?
- What does genuine mastery of each proposed assessment task look like? Do we have credible and appropriate exemplars to anchor our scoring system? Have we justified standards so they are more than local norms?
- Are the test's necessary constraints—imposed-on help available from others, access to resources, time to revise, test secrecy, prior knowledge of standards—authentic?
- Do our assessment tasks have sufficient depth and breadth to allow valid generalizations about overall student competence?
- Have we ensured that the test will not be corrupted by well-intentioned judges of student work?
- Who are the audiences for assessment information, and how should assessment be designed, conducted, and reported to accommodate the needs of each audience?

In terms of format and use most performance tasks fall into three broad categories: short assessment tasks, more ambitious event tasks, and long-term extended tasks.

Short Assessment Tasks

Short assessment tasks are often used to determine how well students have mastered basic concepts, procedures, relationships, and thinking skills within a content area. Generally these tasks take only a few minutes to complete so that several can be combined in a single assessment. Examples of such tasks include open-ended tasks, enhanced multiple-choice questions, and concept mapping.

Most short assessment tasks begin with a **stimulus** designed to set the stage and capture the student's interest. The stimulus might be a problem, cartoon, map, primary source, diagram, or photograph. This is followed by an explanation of the task students are to perform using the stimulus. For example, they might be asked to interpret, describe, calculate, explain, predict, conduct an experiment, or take a position.

Many short assessment tasks also include some amount of **scaffolding,** or information designed to help students frame their response. This might include a bulleted list of key ideas or details that should be included in a response. It might also include a list of the performance criteria by which responses will be judged. In general, scaffolding is intending to foster students' best thinking and writing in their responses.

Open-ended tasks

In **open-ended tasks** students are presented with a stimulus and then asked to communicate an original response. The response might be a brief written answer, a mathematical solution, a drawing, or a diagram. Such tasks may be more or less "open" depending on how many restrictions or directions are included in the scaffolding. Open-ended tasks are also sometimes referred to as *free-response questions.*

Well-designed open-ended tasks present students with a situation that is engaging. They allow students of differing abilities and backgrounds to approach the task in different ways and to follow several paths in framing their response. Below are examples of open-ended tasks in three content areas.

Even after the sale of over one million copies of the *Taxonomy of Educational Objectives–Cognitive Domain* and over a quarter of a century of using this domain in preservice and inservice teacher training, still over 95 percent of test questions that U.S. students are now expected to answer deal with . . . the lowest category of the taxonomy: knowledge.

Benjamin Bloom,
Charles H. Swift
Distinguished Service
Professor,
University of Chicago[8]

Elementary Science Task

Students describe what occurs when a drop of water is placed on each of seven different types of building material. The students then are asked to predict what will happen to a drop of water when it is placed on the surface of an unknown material, which is sealed in a plastic bag so that they can examine but not test it. For this exercise, students need to make careful observations, record findings, and apply what they have learned by hypothesizing what the water will do when placed on an unknown material.

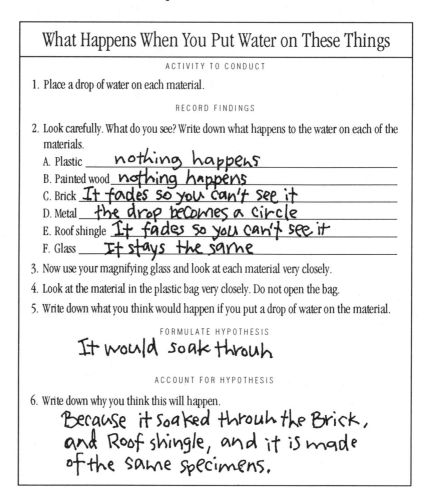

What Happens When You Put Water on These Things

ACTIVITY TO CONDUCT

1. Place a drop of water on each material.

RECORD FINDINGS

2. Look carefully. What do you see? Write down what happens to the water on each of the materials.

   A. Plastic ___nothing happens___
   B. Painted wood ___nothing happens___
   C. Brick ___It fades so you can't see it___
   D. Metal ___the drop becomes a circle___
   E. Roof shingle ___It fades so you can't see it___
   F. Glass ___It stays the same___

3. Now use your magnifying glass and look at each material very closely.

4. Look at the material in the plastic bag very closely. Do not open the bag.

5. Write down what you think would happen if you put a drop of water on the material.

FORMULATE HYPOTHESIS

It would soak throuh

ACCOUNT FOR HYPOTHESIS

6. Write down why you think this will happen.

Because it soaked throuh the Brick, and Roof shingle, and it is made of the same specimens.

Middle School Social Studies Task[10]

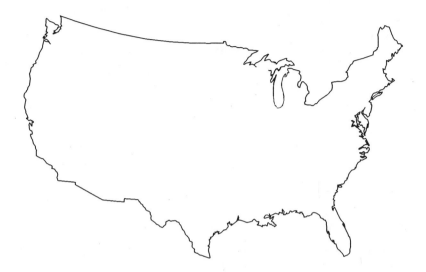

A. *Shade the areas where the 13 colonies were located.*

B. *Label the three groups of colonies: New England colonies, middle colonies, and southern colonies.*

C. *Write a short essay comparing and contrasting the three groups of colonies.*

In your short essay, be sure to tell

- *what the geography and climate of each area was like*

- *how the people in each area made a living*

- *similarities and differences among the three areas*

High School Foreign Language Task[11]

Connecticut has prepared eight forms of this task, one for male and another for female students in German, French, Spanish, and Italian. This form is for male German students.

Directions: *Now that your family has been accepted to host an exchange student in the INTERPALS PROGRAM, write a* *letter in German welcoming the exchange student from Hamburg who is coming to live with you. The student's name is Johann Schmidt. In your letter, write about*

- *your family and the house in which you live*
- *your school and daily activities*
- *your interests and hobbies*
- *something that has happened in your school or community recently*

Ask Johann for any information you would like to know about him, since he is coming to live with you.

Enhanced multiple-choice questions

There are many who question whether the venerable multiple-choice format can ever be made to serve the goals of performance assessment. Tests made up of multiple-choice questions, they maintain, are more likely to measure students' ability to guess than their "knowledge in use."

Others, however, have come to the defense of the multiple-choice question, arguing that if properly constructed it can be an effective and efficient assessment tool. Like other short performance tasks, they say, multiple-choice questions can be designed to assess students' understanding of concepts and higher-order thinking skills.

Out of this debate has emerged the **enhanced multiple-choice question**. Such questions are designed to be more authentic than traditional test items in terms of the problems they present and more challenging in terms of the thinking required to determine the correct response. They can also be made more open-ended by requiring students to explain or justify their responses. The examples below show how multiple-choice questions are being enhanced.

Elementary Mathematics Question[12]

Bill is invited to attend a party given today. His invitation reads:

You are invited to a Birthday Party
Date: April 14
Time: 2:30 p.m.
Place: John's House

Bill has to run an errand for his mom on the way to the party. It will take him 20 minutes. It takes Bill a half hour to get ready for the party and 15 minutes to get to John's house. Bill's watch reads:

Does Bill have enough time to get to the party on time?

A. Bill will be 10 minutes late.

B. Bill will be 5 minutes late.

C. Bill will have 10 extra minutes to get to the party.

D. Bill will have 20 extra minutes to get to the party.

In this period of declining school resources and overcrowded classrooms, multiple-choice testing continues to offer impartiality and an efficient use of teachers' time. With proper effort, we can design multiple-choice questions to test many levels of the cognitive domain.

James Killoran,
Assistant Principal
of Social Studies,
Jamaica High School,
Jamaica, New York[13]

Middle School Science Question[14]

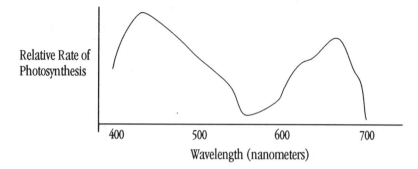

Relative Rate of Photosynthesis

400   500   600   700

Wavelength (nanometers)

Plants get energy for photosynthesis by absorbing light. As shown above, plants photosynthesize at different rates depending upon the wavelength of light they are given. If you were to grow plants under lights of different wavelengths, which of the following wavelengths of light would probably give the best growth?

A. 450 nm   B. 500 nm   C. 550 nm   D. 700 nm

High School Social Studies Question[15]

"For most of the students, this was the greatest danger they had ever faced. . . . Some students could not believe that the army really would use deadly force. But most of all, we were motivated by a powerful sense of purpose. We believed it would be worth sacrificing our lives for the sake of progress and democracy. . . machine guns erupted . . . shooting right at the chests and heads of students. . . ."

The above quote describes

A. the Sepoy Rebellion in India (1857)

B. the Philippine uprising against the Marcos regime (1986)

C. the incident in Tiananmen Square (1989)

D. resistance to the Soviet coup against Gorbachev (1991)

Explain why you chose the answer you did.

Concept mapping

A relatively new assessment tool, **concept mapping** is used to check students' understanding of ideas and relationships. A concept map is a cluster or web of information created by students to represent their understanding of concepts and relationships among ideas. Such maps are constructed by writing the central concept in a circle or oval at the center of a page. Students then note any words and ideas they associate with this concept, using lines and sometimes verbs to indicate relationships between items.

Many teachers find concept mapping particularly useful in culturally diverse classrooms and with students who do not perform well on writing-intensive tasks. Concept maps are also useful for assessing a student's changing understanding of key ideas and relationships over time. The concept maps shown here were made by the same student at the beginning and end of a science unit on light.

Light Unit Concept Maps[16]

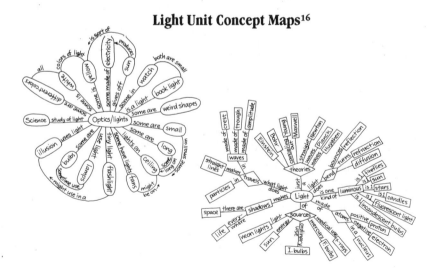

Event Tasks

Event tasks are designed to assess broad competencies such as writing fluency and problem-solving skills. While *event tasks* are often grounded in specific subject areas, they are designed to reveal not only what students know but how well they can put their knowledge to use. Typically these tasks take a period or more to complete.

Unlike short assessment tasks, which are usually done individually, event tasks often involve students working in teams or groups. Evaluation may be based on teacher observations, scoring of students' *performance samples,* self-assessment, peer assessment, or some combination of these approaches.

Reading-writing assessment

A number of states are using event tasks to as part of their reading-writing assessment. Maryland, for example, has developed a three-day integrated reading and writing performance task for its middle school students.[17] During this task, students read a short story and a nonfiction excerpt dealing with a single topic; in one version, the hazards of extreme cold. Then they are asked to integrate what they have learned in a piece of original writing. The sequence of events in this task is as follows:

Day 1: Students begin with a prereading activity that asks them to write a brief journal entry about their own experiences of being cold. Then they read the short story "To Build a Fire" by Jack London, in which the protagonist dies of hypothermia. Students then answer questions designed to assess their understanding of the story and their general reading abilities. At least one question may be answered with a drawing or diagram.

Day 2: Students begin by writing a brief letter to the protagonist of London's short story with advice that might have saved him. A class discussion follows to prepare students for the next reading, an except from a book on hypothermia. During this discussion the teacher creates a cluster diagram of students' ideas as they respond to words they will encounter in their reading. After reading the excerpt, students again answer a series of comprehension questions.

Day 3: Students are asked to integrate information from their reading to write (1) a letter advising a group of friends how to prepare for and safely survive a weekend winter adventure; (2) a poem, story, or short play that captures the writer's feelings about such extreme states as intense cold, heat, hunger, or fatigue; or (3) a speech designed to convince people not to travel to the Yukon. Students begin by brainstorming and recording their ideas either in a list or web. Next they write and revise a rough draft. Finally they use a proofreading guide to help them prepare a final draft.

Evaluation: This performance task is evaluated in two ways. Students' answers to questions are scored to assess reading comprehension. The final written pieces are scored in terms of their effectiveness as persuasive or informative writing.

Process assessment

Process assessment is designed to reveal how well students have mastered a **process** such as clear communication or effective teamwork. While content knowledge may be important in **process assessment** tasks, it is not their central purpose.

Great Britain has designed a number of process assessment tasks that focus on *oracy,* or listening and speaking skills. In a task known as Bridges, for example, one student (the describer) is given a sheet of paper with six pictures of different bridges. A second student (the listener) is given a sheet with pictures of two of the bridges. The first student is to describe each of the six bridges in such detail that the second student can easily determine which two match those on his or her sheet. Speakers in oracy tasks are evaluated in terms of organization of ideas, word choice, syntax, fluency, pacing, and general "orientation to the listener," which includes eye contact and body language.[18]

In the United States many teachers have used **scored dis-cussions** to evaluate group listening and speaking skills. In a scored discussion students receive points, either positive or negative, for their participation in a formal discussion. Often these discussions are held in a ***fishbowl format,*** with the participants gathered in the center of the room and the remaining students and teacher observing from a larger, outer circle. The participants follow a discussion agenda they prepared while researching their topic. As the discussion progresses, the teacher scores each student's contributions on a discussion scoresheet. Scored discussions have been used successfully with students from the primary grades through college. An example of a discussion scoresheet follows.[19]

Sample Discussion Scoresheet			
POSITIVE		NEGATIVE	
Points	*Action*	*Points*	*Action*
2	Taking a position on a question	−2	Not paying attention, or distracting others
1	Making a relevant comment	−2	Interrupting
2	Using evidence to support a position or presenting factual information	−1	Making an irrelevant comment
1	Drawing another person into the discussion	−3	Monopolizing
1	Asking a clarifying question or moving the discussion along	−3	Making a personal attack
2	Making an analogy		
2	Recognizing contradictions		
2	Recognizing irrelevant comments		

Problem-solving and analytical tasks

Event tasks are often used to assess problem-solving and analytical skills. While such tasks vary greatly in their subject matter and complexity, they generally present students with a realistic problem or situation and then ask students to work out a plan, solution, or resolution. Usually the nature of the problem and task is clearly defined. At times, however, students are deliberately presented with an ill-defined problem or incomplete and even confusing information in an effort to make the task more realistic. These two approaches to problem-solving tasks are illustrated below.

Students carry a good deal of anxiety into their first scored discussion. . . . Frequently the most positive students are those who have not succeeded on traditional written research projects.

John Zola,
Social Studies Teacher,
Fairview High School,
Boulder, Colorado[20]

Middle School Mathematics Problem[21]

How many bicycles are there within two miles of this school? Your group's task is to make a plan for investigating this question and to prepare an oral report, with overheads or other displays, for the class. Your planning report is due in three days. Please keep a daily log of your work. Final reports will be due two weeks from today.

High School Economics Problem[22]

You are president of a large company that is facing a major surplus of products you are unable to sell. Will a cutback in production work? Your major task is to get your company into a good financial position. If you are successful, you will be given a large bonus. If you are unsuccessful, you will be fired. Prepare a presentation for your Board of Directors.

1. Market research shows that for every $1 rise in price, 500 fewer units of the product will be demanded. You want to supply 700 units for every dollar rise in price.

- *develop formulas for demand, supply, and equilibrium*

- *graph the company's position*

2. If you are a monopoly, will this change the way you would solve this problem?

3. If you have a surplus:

- *What will happen to your workers?*
- *What will happen to companies that produce complementary products?*

4. If you are forced out of business, what will happen to companies that produce substitute products?

What could this do to the entire economy?

How could the government help in this situation?

Extended Tasks

Extended tasks are long-term, multigoal projects that might be assigned at the beginning of a term or unit of study. Often, activities and milestones are designed into the curriculum to support students as they work through these challenging assignments. Many extended tasks take the form of long-term projects in a specific subject area. Others are designed to be used as rites of passage and exhibitions of mastery at the end of a course of study.

Long-term projects

Long-term projects often serve as the focal point for a unit of study. They create a real-world context for learning and assessment by connecting content to an engaging task. The project illustrated below, for example, asks students to make a video documenting biological succession in their own community. In carrying out this task, students learn about such key concepts as population, habitat, ecological niche, adaptation, and carrying capacity. This extended task was developed in Kentucky and reflects that state's performance assessment goals.

Assessing science through multiple-choice testing is like assessing Larry Bird's basketball skills by asking him to respond to a set of multiple-choice questions.

George E. Hein,
Professor of Liberal Studies and Adult Learning Programs, Lesley College[23]

Documenting Biological Succession Grade 12: Portfolio Task[24]

Goal: ◆ = Main Goal; ◇ = Related Goal(s)

◇	◆	◇	◇	◇	◇
Skill Area	Core Concept(s)	Self-sufficiency	Responsible Group Member	Thinking and Problem Solving	Connecting and Integrating

Core Concept: Patterns

Valued Outcomes: Students identify, compare, and contrast patterns, and use patterns to understand and interpret present events and to predict future events.

Discipline Area: Science

Mode of Presentation: Photo documentary

Technology Requirements: Video camera, 35 mm camera, VCR, TV

Description of Assessment Task: You are a freelance photographer. The production department at Kentucky Education Television (KET) has asked you to develop a 15-minute video documentary about how the biological face of Kentucky is being changed by regional developments (e.g., new highways, shopping centers, subdivisions). You decide to highlight several developments in your own community. As you prepare your documentary, be sure to include several examples of changing habitats and populations as well as expected biological succession that will follow the resulting environmental changes. Point out both good and bad changes that will result. Suggest steps that might be taken to lessen or eliminate the negative changes.

Performance Criteria: The extent to which you

- appropriately collect and display data

- draw accurate conclusions

- depict and explain biological principles, such as habitat, niche, population, and succession

- exhibit originality of work

- display completeness of the work

Source: Kentucky Department of Education

Exhibitions and rites of passage

Exhibitions and rites of passage are culminating activities that demonstrate the accomplishment of major outcomes and mastery of bodies of knowledge. These extended tasks challenge students to show off what they know and what they can do, sometimes on open-ended problems of their own design. Such tasks focus on what Grant Wiggins refers to as:

> *"the essential skills of 'inquiry and expression'—a synthesis that requires questioning, problem posing, problem solving, independent research, the creation of a product or performance, and a* public *demonstration of mastery."*[25]

At Walden III High School in Racine, Wisconsin, students must complete a "Rite of Passage Experience" to receive their diploma. During this year-long project, seniors demonstrate mastery in fifteen areas of knowledge and competence by assembling a portfolio, completing a major research paper, and making a number of oral presentations. The following summary of this extended task was prepared by Grant Wiggins.[26]

Walden III's Rite of Passage Experience (R.O.P.E.)[27]

All seniors must complete a portfolio, a study project on U.S. history, and make fifteen oral and written presentations before a R.O.P.E. committee composed of staff, students, and an outside adult. Nine of the presentations are based on the materials in the portfolio and the project; the remaining six are developed for presentation before the committee. All seniors must enroll in a year-long course designed to help them meet these requirements.

The eight-part *portfolio,* developed in the first semester, is intended to be "a reflection and analysis of the senior's own life and times." The requirements include
- a written autobiography
- a reflection on work (including a résumé)

- an essay on ethics
- a written summary of coursework in science
- an artistic product or a written report on art (including an essay on artistic standards used in judging artwork)

The *project* is a research paper on a topic of the student's choosing in American history. The student is orally questioned on the paper in the presentations before the committee during the second semester.

The *presentations* include oral tests on the previous work, as well as oral and written presentations on subject areas and "personal proficiency" (life skills, setting and realizing personal goals, etc.). The presentations before the committee usually last an hour, with most students averaging about six separate appearances to complete all fifteen presentations.

A diploma is awarded to those students passing twelve of the fifteen presentations and meeting district requirements in math, government, reading, and English.

The In-basket Exercises of Alverno College

Alverno College in Milwaukee, Wisconsin, requires students to exhibit mastery in eight general areas as a condition of graduation:
- effective communication ability
- problem-solving ability
- analytic capability
- effective social interaction
- aesthetic responsiveness
- valuing in a decision-making context
- effective citizenship
- taking responsibility for the global environment[28]

One way Alverno students demonstrate these broad competencies is by undertaking extended tasks known as *in-basket exercises*. In these exercises the student assumes the role of a professional in the community or workplace and then deals with a set of problems that might appear in that person's in basket. Students are to solves these problems under realistic time and information constraints.

In one in-basket exercise, for example, the student takes on the role of a recently hired publications specialist for an urban cultural center.[29] In that role the student is asked to do the following:

- edit an article on the center and cut its length by a third
- deal with an irate citizen who is unhappy with the center's service
- write an editorial responding to a newspaper article that quotes the same irate citizen and identifies him as an activist in a tax reform group promoting government spending cuts
- prepare an outline for a speech to a college class in technical writing.

At the beginning of an in-basket exercise, students are provided with relevant information in the form of memos, dossiers, and reports. They are also expected to draw on their accumulated knowledge and skills to complete their task successfully. Each student's oral and written responses are evaluated by a panel of judges according to specific performance criteria.

Performance assessments like those used at Walden III High School and Alverno College are both time-consuming and labor intensive. The performances they evoke do not lend themselves to easy scoring and reporting of results. Nonetheless, both institutions plan to continue using these extended tasks. The reason may be that in the eyes of both students and teachers, these tasks are tests worth taking.

Opening the Assessment Process to Students and Their Families

6

> *"When people ask, 'What do you do for a living?' I reply, 'I teach writing.' 'Boy, I'll bet you love the red pencil,' they say with innocent admiration. They are pleased to meet a guardian of the public morals."* [1]

When Donald Graves wrote this in 1983, assessment was assumed to be the exclusive domain of teachers and administrators. Armed with red pencils and report cards, they alone were responsible for evaluating student achievement and assigning grades.

One of the aims of the authentic assessment movement is to open up the assessment process to other **stakeholders.** This chapter looks at ways that teachers can share the red pencil with both students and their families.

Student Self-assessment

There are many ways to bring students into the assessment process, as well as reasons for doing so. Teachers who make self-and peer evaluation a routine part of their assessment program find they no longer have to correct and grade every paper a student produces. More important, when students take on increased responsibility for evaluating their own and each other's work, they begin to internalize performance standards and to

> It's . . . sad seeing educators taking on all the burden of evaluation themselves . . . when they could be sharing that responsibility with learners and their parents.
>
> ***David Dillon,***
> *Editor,* Language Arts [2]

apply them to future efforts. With this increase in autonomy comes a sense of ownership of one's own learning and growth.

Students can begin to develop the habit of self-assessment very early. A kindergarten teacher at Blackburn Elementary School in Manatee County, Florida, discovered this for herself when she posted a scale of children's writing development on a bulletin board in her classroom. The teacher explained to her students how writing develops in stages and suggested that they might want to determine where their own work fit on the scale. To her amazement, most of her kindergartners identified the level of their work quite accurately. Using their new understanding of the writing process, many students began to take more risks in their work.[3]

Collaborative goal setting

In many classrooms, collaborative assessment begins with collaborative goal setting. In this process, teachers and students work together to establish their instructional goals in each subject area for the year. Once identified, these goals are posted in the classroom where they can be referred to as often as needed. From time to time throughout the year, students are asked both individually and collectively to reflect on their progress towards the class goals. The list below is an example of a mathematics class's goals for the year.

Our goals for this year[5]

- Understanding the mathematics we do
- Cooperating and respecting each other
- Being open to new ideas and new approaches
- Explaining mathematical ideas clearly
- Thinking visually
- Reasoning and thinking about problems
- Having self-esteem and self-confidence
- Being able to keep working on a problem

Evaluative questions and starter sentences

Evaluative questions are the basic tools of self-assessment. They ask students to stop and reflect on what they are doing. They also encourage metacognition, or thinking about how we think and learn.

Sample Evaluative Questions

What was hardest about writing today?
Is there another way we could solve this problem?
What goals did you set for yourself in this piece?
What do you think you should do next?
What would you do differently if you could do this again?
Why did you choose this for your portfolio?
What did you learn doing this assignment?
What new questions did this activity raise?

Teachers who want to encourage self-assessment use evaluative questions frequently in conversations with individual students and in group discussions. Many teachers also make such questions the focus of **journal** or **learning log** entries, often by turning them into starter sentences like the ones below.

Sample Starter Sentences

Today in math I learned _____
When I get stuck writing, I _____
What I still don't understand about electricity is _____
The thing I am most proud of doing this week is _____
The problem-solving strategy I used today was_____
My goals for myself as a writer are _____

Assessment forms and checklists

Assessment forms and checklists are also useful tools for helping students to evaluate their own and each other's work. This problem-solving checklist was developed by the British Colombia Ministry of Education for self-assessment in math.

We must become more flexible in our assessment of students' work. . . .When we trust them to set goals and to evaluate their learning in progress, we will begin to realize that they know much more than we allow them to tell us through our set curriculums and standardized tests.

Linda Rief,
Teacher, Oyster River
Middle School,
Durham, New Hampshire[6]

Problem-Solving Strategy Inventory[7]

Think about your use of strategies when solving the problem and check the following that apply.

1. __ I didn't think about using strategies at all.
2. __ The idea of using strategies came to my mind, but I didn't think about it much more.
3. __ I looked at a strategy list, but didn't try a strategy.
4. __ I looked at a strategy list and picked a strategy, which I tried.
5. __ I didn't look at a list, but just thought of a strategy to try.
6. __ I used at least one strategy and it helped me find a solution.
7. __ I tried the following strategies:

   ____ guess and check   ____ solve a simpler problem
   ____ make a table   ____ work backward
   ____ look for a pattern   ____ draw a picture
   ____ make an organized list   ____ write an equation
   ____ other _____

Many teachers develop assessment forms collaboratively with their students. The form on page 63 was created by a third-grade class to assess their persuasive writing.[8] It was designed to bring together self-assessment, peer assessment, and teacher assessment on one page.

Peer assessment

Informal peer assessment takes place in every classroom. Students naturally look at each other's work, note what is valued and praised by their friends, and look at the samples that teachers display in order to determine what is acceptable and appropriate. Some students may even lower the quality of their work to match peer standards.

Evaluation Sheet

For writing to convince (Person): __Mom and Dad__

Author __Chris__   Partner __Meg__

	author	partner	Mrs. R.
PERSUASION			
What I want the reader to do is clear. _Not walk my sister to school._	✓	✓	✓
There are logical reasons given. _Yes!_	✓	✓	✓
There is evidence that I know the reader and have anticipated and answered problems or arguments the reader may have.	✓	✓	✓
CONVENTIONS			
Paragraphs are used for separate ideas.	✓	✓	✓
Punctuation follows our rules sheet. (ending punctuation, commas, (apostrophes)) ← _fix_	✓	–	✓
Capital letters are used where needed.	✓	✓	✓
Words are circled that may be misspelled. (draft)	✓	✓	✓
Words are spelled correctly. (final copy)	✓	✓	✓
Handwriting meets our standards for writing that will be read by others.	✓	✓	✓
WRITING PROCESS			
I told my partner all about the person who had to be convinced.	✓	✓	
I tried out my persuasion with my partner.	✓	✓	
I told my response group what to listen for.	✓	✓	
I considered the comments and questions of my response group.	✓		
I listened and reacted as the person to be convinced when other kids read their letters.	✓		
REVISION HELP			
The purpose sentence is underlined in red. The reason sentences are underlined in blue. The anticipation of problem sentences are in green.	✓	✓	✓

A number of techniques have been developed to make peer assessment a more formal part of the assessment process. One is the practice of having students formally critique each others' work. During a critiquing session, the students being evaluated present works-in-progress, explaining what they are trying to achieve and how. Fellow students then offer detailed feedback on what seems to be working and what might be improved.

Another technique is the evaluation of teamwork skills and individual contributions to group activities. The peer score sheet shown below was developed to assess group work in science, but could easily be adapted to other subjects. This form is designed to help each student identify his or her strengths and weaknesses as a team worker, while reminding students that individuals can make different kinds of contributions to team efforts. At the same time, teachers can use the information provided by students for both grading and grouping purposes.

Peer Score Sheet (scores as percentages)[9]

STUDENTS	Ana	Rob	Lauren	Aran
Creativity/Ideas	50	20	30	0
Research/Data Collection	20	10	10	60
Writing/Typing/Artwork	0	10	60	30
Organizing/Collating	20	0	50	30
Total Percent Contribution	22	10	38	30

Comments: *Lauren helped me a lot on this project. Ana had a lot of good ideas.*

The Family's Role in Assessment

The opening of the assessment process has created new opportunities and roles for the families of students. In the past, families have been viewed primarily as passive recipients of assessment information. This is beginning to change as schools invite family members to become involved in assessment as providers of information and feedback and as active participants in the assessment process.

Providers of information

Schools have traditionally asked family members to provide only the most basic information about students: address, phone numbers, legal guardian, health data, and names of siblings. Some schools, however, are now reaching out to families for more detailed information about a student's interests, attitudes toward school, learning styles, special problems, and so on. This information can be gathered in conferences or from questionnaires.

Audience for student work

Family members have always made up much of the audience at school concerts, plays, and athletic events. That role is now being expanded as families are being asked to become part of a widening audience for student work in language arts, mathematics, science, social studies, and art. Some schools encourage students to bring their work to a larger audience through newsletters sent home to families.

Schools are also inviting family members to review and reflect on student's work on a regular basis. Often this is done by sending work home in a portfolio and asking a family member for a written response. For many families, this truly is an eye-opening experience. The portfolio review form shown below was developed by Kathryn Howard, a teacher in Pittsburgh's Arts PROPEL program, when she found that her students needed a

> When we report progress to parents we also accept the responsibility to share with them the new views about reading, writing, problem solving, and learning.
>
> **Ron Hutchison,**
> *Principal, Jackson Elementary School, Hillsboro School District, Oregon*[11]

larger audience for their writing. After reading how family members responded to their work, students made comments like "My parents now know that I do take my work seriously and that I can be creative sometimes" and "The thing that surprised me most is that she really liked it."[12]

Parent Portfolio Review[13]

Reader's Name _____ Date _____

Student's Name _____

Please read everything in your child's writing folder, including drafts and commentary. Each piece is set up in back-to-front order, from rough draft to final copy. Further, each piece is accompanied by both student and teacher comments on the piece and the writing process. Finally, the folders also include written questionnaires where students write about their strengths and weaknesses as writers.

We believe that the best assessment of student writing begins with the students themselves, but must be broadened to include the widest possible audience. We encourage you to become part of the audience.

When you have read the folders, please talk to your children about their writing. In addition, please take a few minutes to respond to these questions.

- Which piece of writing in the folder tells you the most about your child's writing?

- What does it tell you?

- What do you see as the strengths in your child's writing?

- What do you see as needing to be addressed in your child's growth and development as a writer?

- What suggestions do you have that might aid the class's growth as writers?

- Other comments, suggestions?

Thank you so much for investing this time in your child's writing.

Volunteer assessment aides

One concern often heard about authentic assessment is that it is too labor- and time-intensive for overworked teachers to manage. Some school districts are looking at ways to reduce the time burden on teachers by using volunteers as data gatherers and evaluators.

Longfellow Elementary School in Bozeman, Montana, has successfully involved volunteers in the assessment of its Art in Action program. Twice a year volunteers interview every student in grades one through four about a work of art and score the results. The process and questions used in the interview were designed by a committee of parents, teachers, and the school principal. Volunteer interviewers are then trained to ensure uniformity of scoring. One enthusiastic volunteer says of the art assessment:

> *"In the past students were graded simply on their ability to draw. This new assessment centers around evaluating a student's knowledge of the properties of art: not everyone can draw—but everyone can enjoy art. I like it."*[14]

Opening the assessment process may not always generate such enthusiasm. But it can ease the assessment burden now borne mainly by teachers by harnessing the energy of students and their families in productive ways. More important, encouraging students and their families to become collaborators in assessment is a powerful way of communicating the school's expectations and standards. That alone should convince teachers and administrators to share the red pencil.

Scoring and Grading
the New Assessments

7

In August 1992, forty teachers gathered at a hotel in San Diego, California, to score the results of a new open-ended social studies assessment. This being a pilot year, only 5,000 eighth-grade students had taken the three-day test. Still, the task of reading and grading so many written responses seemed overwhelming at first. Social studies teacher Frank Huyette described the daily grind this way:

> *"You get up and have breakfast and grade papers and have lunch and grade papers and have dinner and never want to look at another paper again. And the next day you start all over again."*

By the end of four days, however, every paper had been read and scored by two teachers. Significant differences of opinion about scores had been resolved by a third reading. This scoring system, commented Huyette, "may not be totally accurate. But it gives us a good sense of what our students can do."[1]

For years we have relied on machines to attach numbers to large-scale assessments. As we shift to authentic assessment, however, human beings will have to take over that role. In this chapter we will look at how teachers and assessment programs are stepping up to that challenge.

New Scoring Tools

Assessments based on observations, portfolios, and performance tasks cannot be scored like standardized tests. A machine is not capable of evaluating an individual student's musical performance, science project, or writing portfolio and coming up with a precise score. Such evaluations will be have to be made by human beings.

This reliance on human evaluators raises questions about the costs and time involved in scoring authentic assessments. It also raises concerns about the reliability and consistency of scores based on human judgment. In an effort to deal with these concerns, new scoring tools and methods are being developed to go along with the new assessments.

Scoring rubrics

For human judgments to be considered something more trustworthy than mere opinion, they must be based on clearly articulated standards. Scoring rubrics are one way of communicating those standards to the various stakeholders in assessment—teachers, students, family members, administrators, and so on.

A *rubric* is an established set of criteria used for scoring or rating students' tests, portfolios, or performances. A scoring rubric describes the levels of performance students might be expected to attain relative to a desired standard of achievement. These *descriptors,* or performance descriptions, tell the evaluator what characteristics or signs to look for in a student's work and then how to place that work on a predetermined *scale.*

The following example of a scoring rubric was designed by teachers in Texas to measure and score elementary science students' performance in the task of drawing conclusions based on experimental data.[2]

Sample Rubric: Drawing Conclusions

Points	Characteristics
0	Fails to reach a conclusion
1	Draws a conclusion that is not supported by data
2	Draws a conclusion that is supported by data, but fails to show any evidence for the conclusion
3	Draws a conclusion that is supported by the data and gives supporting evidence for the conclusion.

A simple rubric such as this combines several virtues. It communicates quite clearly what standard of achievement is desired. It creates a scoring system that is easy to learn and use. By describing specific and observable performance characteristics, it reduces the likelihood of inaccurate scoring. It also helps students to assess where they are on the achievement scale and how they might improve their performance. Finally, it can be used repeatedly throughout the year to document a pattern of performance and progress.

Benchmarks

Scoring rubrics are often supplemented by **benchmarks**, or performance samples that serve as a concrete standard against which other samples may be judged. Generally a benchmark is provided for each achievement level in a scoring rubric.

The Ontario Ministry of Education and Toronto Board of Education have made extensive use of benchmarks in their performance-based language arts and mathematics assessment programs. The examples below illustrate the range of student responses to a mathematics performance task. In this task third-grade students were asked to create and write a mathematical problem based on their choice of a picture; in this case, one of six dogs. Students were told they did not have to solve the problem they wrote. The responses were scored on a five-point scale. Shown here are descriptors and benchmarks for levels five and three.[4]

It is easier to propose outcomes than it is to set the criteria and establish the performance levels.

Gene I. Maeroff,
Senior Fellow, Carnegie
Foundation for the
Advancement of Teaching[3]

Level Five: The student writes a multi-step problem that involves more than one mathematical operation. The story problem is logical and creative, realistically relates to the picture, and allows a numerical solution. If units (e.g. dollars) are worked into the story, they are appropriately chosen and used. The student's control of standard written English does not interfere with reading the problem.

Level Five
there were 6 dogs 2 are pregnent each dog is having nine babies   how many dogs (inclouding the six others,) are there all together

Once upon a time there was no water. So I took my Bow and arrow and tied a rope on my arrow and shoot it where the stars were. The arrow caught on the stars and I pulled until the Big Dipper tilted enough to spill out water, and that is how we have water now.

Vermont Grade 4 Portfolio Assessment Benchmark Paper illustrating writing that frequently exhibits proper usage, mechanics, and grammar[5]

Level Three: The student writes a one-step story problem that can be solved easily. One-digit numbers are usually used. The student may present the information and various elements of the problem without properly stating a mathematical problem. The student's control of standard English may interfere with reading the problem.

Level Three
there are 6 dogs and one of them walked away how meny are left?

Holistic scoring

Using scoring rubrics and benchmarks, evaluators generally score student work in one of two ways. The first method is **holistic scoring,** scoring based on an overall impression of a sample of student work looked at as a whole. Holistic scoring produces a single number, typically based on a four- to six-point scale, and is used when a relatively quick yet consistent scoring method is needed, as with many large-scale assessments.

The holistic rubric shown on page 74 was developed by the California Assessment Program to help teachers score solutions to an open-ended math problem.[6]

Analytic Scoring

The second method used with the new assessments is **analytic scoring.** This approach involves the awarding of separate scores for different traits or **dimensions** of a student's work. When the traits being emphasized are specific to a certain genre of writing or type of task, this method may be called **primary trait scoring.**

While analytic scoring is more time-consuming than holistic scoring, it also yields more detailed information. For that reason it is often used for diagnostic purposes or when students need specific feedback on their strengths and weaknesses. Analytic scoring is also used to evaluate curriculum and instructional programs and to pinpoint areas in need of improvement.

Holistic Scoring Rubric

Problem: James knows that half the students from his school are accepted at the public university nearby. Also, half are accepted at the local private college. James thinks that these figures add up to 100 percent, so he will surely be accepted at one or the other institution. Explain why James may be wrong. If possible use a diagram in your explanation.

4 points: Exemplary response
All the following characteristics must be present:
- The answer is correct.
- The explanation is clear and complete.
- The explanation includes a mathematically correct reason for the faulty reasoning involving the assumption of disjoint sets in the problem.
- Some sort of diagram is provided that relates directly and correctly to the information in the problem.

3 points: Good response
Exactly one of the following characteristics is present.
- The answer is incorrect.
- The explanation lacks clarity.
- The explanation is incomplete.
- No diagram is provided that relates directly and correctly to the information in the problem.

2 points: Inadequate response
All the following characteristics must be present:
- The answer is incorrect.
- The explanation lacks clarity or is incomplete but does indicate some correct and relevant reasoning.
- No diagram is provided that relates directly and correctly to the information in the problem.

1 point: Poor response
All the following characteristics must be present:
- The answer is incorrect.
- The explanation, if any, uses irrelevant arguments (e.g., whether a student is qualified for college, whether a student has applied for college).
- No solution is attempted beyond just copying data given in the problem statement.
- No diagram is provided that relates directly and correctly to the information in the problem.

0 points: No response
- The student's paper is blank or it contains only work that appears to have no relevance to the problem.

Vermont uses analytic scoring in its statewide portfolio writing assessment. **Raters** use a detailed analytic assessment guide to evaluate the work collected in portfolios along five different dimensions.[8] The work in each portfolio is scored according to whether it exhibits each of these traits extensively, frequently, sometimes, or rarely. Benchmark papers assist the rater in making this judgment. The five dimensions Vermont uses to score student writing are

- clarity of purpose and awareness of audience
- organization and coherence
- appropriate use of details
- distinctive voice and tone
- correct usage, mechanics, and grammar

Verifying assessment results

For these new scoring methods to gain acceptance, they must produce consistent, reliable, and meaningful results. One way to monitor scoring consistency is through sampling.

Vermont uses sampling to ensure the integrity of its statewide portfolio-based writing assessment program. Student portfolios are initially scored by each child's classroom teacher, working individually or cooperatively with other teachers. Teachers evaluate the portfolios using an analytic scoring rubric provided by the state. The resulting scores are used by teachers for diagnostic, grading, instructional, and other purposes, and by the state to evaluate Vermont's writing program.

In late spring each teacher brings a sample of five portfolios to a regional meeting for teachers from several schools to evaluate. The results of these regional assessments are then compared to the in-school results to determine the reliability of scoring. A sample of portfolios from each regional meeting is scored again at a statewide meeting to ensure that common standards are being applied statewide. This process of collectively establishing and maintaining standards is known as **moderation.**

Critics are correct when they say performance assessment will take more time and teacher training than do multiple-choice tests. But that may make them more effective. To score a writing sample, for example, teachers have to really understand the process of writing. . . . They will no longer rely on pat phrases like "Good description!" or "Nice ending!"

Krista Ramsey,
Education Columnist[7]

Another approach to verification is to have someone **audit,** or recheck, the design and scoring of assessments to assure that the desired achievement standards are being met. This may be done informally by having teachers from different subject areas, grade levels, or schools cross-read and critique samples from other teachers' assessment programs. A more formal approach is to appoint an audit committee made up of teachers, administrators, assessment experts, family members, business people, and other community representatives to evaluate assessment results.

Group Grading

An often-voiced concern about using human beings to score assessments is that individual judgments are bound to be subjective, even biased. One way to guard against bias in large-scale assessments is to insist on **blind scoring,** or the grading of student work without the knowledge of who produced the work.

Group grading is another means of reducing subjectivity, in this case by replacing a single subjective judgment with a consensus of many judgments. In this process, individual scoring quirks tend to be minimized or even eliminated. The participants in a group grading session are generally teachers who meet to score large numbers of portfolios, performance samples, or tests. Depending on the workload, the grading session might take just a day or stretch out for a week.

Training

Group grading begins with a training period during which the participants learn to rate performances, papers, or portfolios according to a set of agreed-upon standards. Usually the graders work in teams, each headed by an experienced leader.

The first priority of the group is to come to agreement on the standards by which student work will be judged. To begin this process, each person is given the same set of sample papers to grade. The samples are selected in advance to illustrate the full

Instead of sending the tests to a commercial firm for scoring, teachers will be trained and paid to do it. The students will be responsible for the work. The profession will be responsible for assessing that work.

Richard P. Mills,
Vermont Commissioner
of Education[9]

range of student achievement on the assessment. The graders may be guided by an existing scoring rubric. If not, they will need to develop a rubric during the training period.

After scoring the samples individually, team members meet together for **calibration.** This involves comparing initial scores, identifying areas of disagreement, and then working toward consensus. As part of this process the graders explore exactly what the standards they used to assign scores mean. They also confront possible biases, such as an aversion to misspelled words or nonstandard English. Calibration continues until the entire group reaches agreement on the score for each sample. At that point, the samples can serve as *anchor papers,* or benchmarks for scoring other papers.

Scoring

With scoring standards fresh in everyone's mind, the group turns to the task of evaluating student papers or work samples. Generally each paper is scored twice, with neither reader knowing the other's score. If the two scores are close, they are aggregated to make up a final grade. If there is a significant discrepancy, a third person, usually the team leader, grades the paper again to resolve the differences.

A number of moderation techniques have been developed to insure consistency of scoring across a group. One is to have team leaders routinely select and reread already scored papers to make sure that standards are being applied in the same way by all team members. Another is to circulate papers already scored by one team to other teams to see if the papers receive the same scores. A third is to pause one or twice a day for group calibration during which everyone reads the same paper and comes to an agreement on how it should be scored.

Teachers who participate in group grading generally report that it is an intense but rewarding experience. One reason may be that in these sessions they address the most fundamental questions of teaching: What do we value and why? And how can we judge whether or not our students are reflecting those values in their work?

What About Grades?

Another concern often raised about authentic assessment is that it will make grading more complicated, time consuming, or just plain difficult. Correcting objective tests is easier than scoring performance tasks or portfolios. In evaluating such open-ended works teachers have to make difficult judgment calls. For example, how much should effort count in assessing a portfolio? Should a student response be accepted even if it is written in nonstandard English? Should all members of a team receive the same score on a performance task regardless of their input?

Authentic assessment challenges teachers to change how students are evaluated. This section looks at how two writing teachers met that challenge when they put portfolio assessment at the center of their grading systems.

A portfolio/conference grading system

The year she started having students in her junior high school writing classes create portfolios, Jane Hancock attended a conference on portfolio assessment the last Saturday of the semester. At one point the person sitting next to her leaned over and whispered, "If I opened your grade book right now, what would I see." "Nothing," Hancock whispered back, "except absences and tardies."

When Hancock had implemented portfolio assessment earlier in the year, she stopped putting grades on assignments and in her gradebook. Instead she began annotating each paper with comments and suggestions for improvement.

Toward the end of the quarter, Hancock met with students individually to review their portfolios. In preparation for these conferences, she asked students to write her a letter in which they identified their best pieces and discussed how they had grown as writers. "I enjoyed their letters," Hancock reported afterward. "I grinned when they pointed out their use of strong verbs, the fact that they had 'shown' not 'told,' that they had 'cut the fat.' Some had even highlighted words and sentences and paragraphs where revision had occurred, so I could find them easily."

During portfolio conferences, Hancock reviews with students their entire body of work. They discuss grades, which Hancock bases on effort, improvement, style, attention to mechanics, and completeness. By the time she finishes these conferences, Hancock knows each student's work and course grade.

Since implementing this portfolio/conference grading system, Hancock reports, "no one has questioned or contested a grade." Just as important, she notes, students have more to show for themselves at the end of the semester than a letter grade. "Portfolios speak to the parent, to the teacher, to the administration. Most importantly, they speak to the student as a writer."[12]

The nice thing about portfolios is that they can literally fit into any grading scheme that is being currently used.

Mark A. Carter,
Elementary Teacher,
Upper Arlington,
Ohio School District [11]

An adaptable portfolio grading system

Margie Krest writes that when she shifted to portfolio assessment in her high school writing classes, four things happened.

1. I lightened my paper load.
2. I began spending most of each semester coaching rather than grading students.
3. I began looking forward to grading students' papers (at least I became excited about how an idea or revision turned out).
4. Most important, I watched as previously unmotivated writers became motivated to work for a grade they desired and at the same time to improve their writing.[13]

Krest assesses portfolios every four to eight weeks, depend-ing on the level of the students and their needs. If her primary goal for students is to develop fluency, she might give them a full quarter to work at becoming more fluent before assessing their work. If her goal is to encourage revision, she assesses more often to provide feedback on specific problems students should attend to during the revision process.

Rather than assessing everything students write, Krest spends her time on those pieces students edit, revise, and con-fer about. This approach grows out of her belief that "students need the freedom to fail, abandon an idea, or just practice with different techniques."[14]

Krest gives students two grades on their portfolios. The first is a portfolio grade based on the amount of revision and risk-taking shown in the entire body of work. The second mark is a final product grade assigned to just one piece in the portfolio. This grade is based on Krest's own rubric of high-order con-cerns (organization, focus, development, tone, voice), middle-order concerns (style, sentence structure, sentence variety), and low-order concerns (punctuation, word usage, spelling).

Krest adapts her portfolio grading system to different classes and skill levels by assigning the two portfolio grades different weights before combining them for a final grade.

> "If I want to emphasize fluency, risk taking, and revision,
> I weight the portfolio grade 60% to 75% and weight the
> final paper grade only 25–40%. In this way, lower-level
> students who often struggle to overcome writing problems
> do not get discouraged if their 'final product grade' isn't
> an A or B. They know that if they work in 'good faith'. . .
> they can actually do quite well in their writing classes."[16]

With her most advanced students, Krest reverses the weight-ing to put more emphasis on the final product. The results, she reports, have been spectacular.

"They now work to change average to above-average papers, which they would have settled for in the past, into meaningful essays that they proudly display at the end of the quarter. They are challenged to use their already developed workshop skills to realize their full potential as writers."[17]

As the experiences of both Hancock and Krest illustrate, authentic assessment does not necessarily make grading more difficult. Instead, the new assessments can help us ensure that grades reflect our highest goals for students. In making such a determination, there is no substitute for the thoughtful judgment of the classroom teacher.

Implementing Authentic Assessments

8

When Inez Fugate Liftig decided to experiment in her eighth-grade science classes with new assessments that emphasized open-ended, interpretive questions she ran into problems. All too often her students handed in papers with questions left unanswered or with responses so incomplete or general that they had no meaning. "In most cases," Liftig found, "these students know the answer, but they do not know how to correctly answer the question."[1]

Liftig's students had trouble with her new assessments for several reasons. Conditioned by years of multiple-choice testing, they were not used to reading questions carefully and thoughtfully before answering. Nor did most of her students know how to respond to such directives as *compare, summarize, define, state, analyze,* and *evaluate.* When students were able to construct responses, they often left out key information on the assumption that their teacher already knew the material. Only after addressing these problems was Liftig able to make her new approach to assessment fly.

As Liftig discovered, implementing a new assessment program may not be an easy or straightforward task. A change in assessment practices often necessitates other changes in what is taught and how. This chapter looks at some of the questions, issues, and concerns that are part of this process of change.

Identifying the Central Issues

Creating a new assessment program is a messy, time-consuming process. There exists no neat blueprint or one-size-fits-all plan for implementing authentic assessments—whether on a state, district, school, or classroom basis—and that is probably just as well. If what you test is indeed what you get, then any change in assessment should be the result of thoughtful planning.

The first step in that planning process is to identify the central issues involved in developing a new assessment plan. Some of those issues are listed below in the form of questions. Still others are likely to emerge as planning proceeds and new assessments are implemented. The questions that typically arise when developing a new assessment program range from philosophical issues such as the purpose of assessment to practical concerns such as how to organize the planning process.

The planning process

- Who should be part of the planning process?
- How should that process be structured?
- What models, standards, and criteria can be identified to help guide the planning process?

Purpose and focus

- What is the purpose of creating a new assessment program?
- Who is to be evaluated and why?
- What key objectives and outcomes are to be assessed?
- Should the main focus of assessments be formative, summative, or both?
- Should assessments document competence at a given moment, growth over time, or both?
- Who will use this information and how?

Assessment strategies

- What assessment strategies are most likely to serve the purposes of the new assessment program?

- Are those strategies fair to students of different learning styles, abilities, genders, and cultural backgrounds?
- How will the new assessment strategies be integrated into the curriculum?
- What resources are needed to implement these strategies?

Scoring issues

- How will assessments be scored or graded?
- What should be considered evidence of achievement of key objectives and outcomes?
- How will consistency and objectivity of scoring be maintained?
- Should moderation efforts be undertaken so that local scores will be comparable to those of other localities?

Verification and reporting

- What verification and audit procedures should be implemented to ensure the validity and reliability of assessments?
- How should assessment information be organized and reported?

Planning and Implementing Change

Planning and implementing a new assessment program on any scale can be a lengthy and complex task. Change may originate with a few teachers who decide to experiment with new assessment ideas, or it may be part of a school or district effort to revamp assessment practices.

Whatever the scale of change, the process of developing new assessments is often more evolutionary than revolutionary. Such was the case when the San Dieguito Union High School district in California implemented portfolio assessment in all English classes during the 1991–92 school year. This change came only after a three-year long process of planning and field-testing.[3] During this period, the focus of planning shifted from the creation of a uniform portfolio design to a more individualized, teacher-controlled approach. According to Assistant Superintendent Donald Kemp and teacher Winfield Cooper:

> *"Each stage of this process took time. Had we hastily institutionalized the first model we came up with, we might not have explored other possibilities and it is unlikely that we would have achieved the degree of teacher buy-in necessary to make portfolios a meaningful part of everyone's English class."*[4]

Advice for administrators

Planning and implementing a new assessment program takes time, attention, patience, and perseverance. For administrators about to embark on this adventure, the following advice from veterans of assessment reform may prove helpful.

1. *Avoid the temptation to import and implement a ready-made assessment program without extensive teacher consultation.* Unless teachers buy into and support the new program, it is not likely to succeed.

2. *Identify and recruit teacher-leaders to head the planning process.* Such leaders may be department chairs, mentor teachers, or teachers with a special interest in assessment reform. One way to feed this interest is to encourage teachers to attend workshops or classes on new methods of instruction in their content areas. Teachers' enthusiasm for changing assessment often grows out of the realization that new ways of teaching their subject require new forms of evaluation.

3. *Promote as much teacher involvement and collaboration as possible in every phase of the planning process.* Extensive collaboration encourages a genuine sense of ownership in the new assessment plan. Without this sense of involvement, teachers may not be highly motivated to change their assessment practices.

4. *Recognize the critical connection between curriculum, teaching practices, and assessment as you plan and implement your new assessment program.* A change in one area inevitably affects the other two. Such effects should be the result of conscious design rather than unwelcome surprises.

5. *Encourage continued teacher collaboration once the program is in place.* Teachers will need time for collegial sharing and fine-tuning as they gain experience with the new assessment program.

6. *Expect that your new assessment program will cost more than traditional forms of assessment and budget accordingly.* Your new program may necessitate additional spending on storage space for portfolios, on equipment for performance tasks, and on photocopying machines for teachers. You may also need funds to support teacher in-service training, planning time, and group-grading sessions.

7. *Learn to view change as a process, not an event.* People need time to adapt to change. By planning for a staged implementation, your staff can make the necessary adjustments and refinements along the way to make the new program work as planned.

Tips for teachers

For teachers planning to implement some form of authentic assessment in their classrooms, with or without district support, the following tips from the trenches may help you get started.

1. *Establish your own personal evaluation plan.* This plan should be based on your instructional goals, teaching strategies, and information needs. It should identify the assessment strategies that you think are workable in your classroom and that will generate information appropriate to your goals and needs.

The use of alternative forms of assessment may mean decentralization of a school district's testing program so that assessment can become an instructional activity integrated into the daily classroom routine.

*Janet L. McDaid,
Director of Testing,
Evaluation and Research,
Whittier Union
High School District
Donna G. Davis,
Program Evaluation
Manager,
San Diego City Schools*[5]

2. *Share your plan with students.* Your plan is far more likely to succeed if you make your students collaborators in the assessment process. Discuss your goals and expectations openly with students and elicit their feedback and ideas.

3. *Start small.* You don't have to implement all of your evaluation plan at once. Begin with one or two new ideas. Give your students and yourself time to become comfortable with these assessment techniques before introducing more changes.

4. *Make assessment part of your daily class routine.* Most teachers worry about finding time to implement new assessment techniques in their already hectic schedule. Those who have done so successfully say that the secret is to integrate assessment into other classroom activities as much as possible.

5. *Set up an easy and efficient record-keeping system.* As your means of assessment change, you will need more than a gradebook to capture the resulting assessment data. Record-keeping options include a loose-leaf notebook, a card file, file folders, or a computer data base. In designing your system, consider ways that students can help you with record keeping.

Evaluating the Results

Once a new assessment program has been planned and implemented, how should it be evaluated? By what standards should assessment programs be judged? Should the same standards apply to at the classroom, district, state, and even national level?

In November of 1991 the National Center for Fair and Open Testing invited more than twenty education, civil rights, and advocacy organizations to meet and consider these and other questions arising out of the assessment revolution. Participants included representatives from the Association for Supervision and Curriculum Development, the Children's Defense Fund, the

True standards of intellect—even those of a restless, noisy adolescent—do not lend themselves wholly to quickly collected, precise, standard measurement. We need to devise clusters of instruments (to use a bloodless but apt word) to probe our students' ability to think resourcefully about important things. Indeed, we need time to reflect deeply on what we mean by "think resourcefully" and what we feel are the most "important things."

Theodore R. Sizer,
Dean of Graduate School
of Education,
Brown University[6]

Center for Women's Policy Studies, the National Science Teacher's Association, and the NAACP. This coalition called itself the National Forum on Assessment and set itself the task of developing standards for assessment programs.

After "strenuous discussion of assessment as a part of the education system," the Forum reached consensus on eight criteria every assessment program should meet. These criteria address the key issues in assessment, beginning with standards and purpose and moving on to fairness, validity, teacher involvement, and reporting. The Forum says of this effort:

> *"We see the Criteria being used to judge both old and new assessment systems, but we do not see them as a panacea. No one thing in education will alone work miracles. Teachers need professional development to help them meet curriculum standards, schools need infusions of technology to prepare students for the world they will live in, and students need individual help. . . so that they can realize their potential. When implemented, our small contribution will remove an obstacle by ensuring that assessment supports everyone's best efforts."[7]*

Criteria for Evaluation of Student Assessment Systems[8]

1. *Educational standards specifying what students should know and be able to do should be clearly defined before assessment procedures and exercises are developed.*
   "For assessment information to be valid and useful, assessment must be based on a consensus definition of what students are expected to learn, and the expected level of performance, at various developmental stages. . . . The standards should be determined through open discussion among subject-matter experts, educators, parents, policymakers, and others, including those concerned with the relationship between school learning and life outside of school."

2. *The primary purpose of the assessment systems should be to assist both educators and policymakers to improve instruction and advance student learning.*

   "Students, educators, parents, policymakers, and others have . . . different uses for assessment information. For example, teachers, students and their parents want information on individual achievement, while policymakers and the public want information for accountability purposes. In all cases, the system should be designed to provide not just numbers or ratings, but useful information on the particular abilities students have or have not developed."

3. *Assessment standards, tasks, procedures, and uses should be fair to all students.*

   "Assessment tasks and procedures must be sensitive to cultural, racial, class and gender differences, and to disabilities, and must be valid for and not penalize any groups. To ensure fairness, students should have multiple opportunities to meet standards and should be able to meet them in different ways."

4. *The assessment exercises or tasks should be valid and appropriate representations of the standards students are expected to achieve.*

   "A sound assessment system provides information about a full range of knowledge and abilities considered valuable and important for students to learn, and therefore requires a variety of assessment methods."

5. *Assessment results should be reported in the context of other relevant information.*

   "Information about student performance should be one part of a system of multiple indicators of the quality of education. Multiple indicators permit educators and policymakers to examine the relationships among *context factors* (such as the type of community, socioeconomic status of students, and school climate), *resources* (such as expenditures per student, physical plant, staffing, and money for materials and equipment), *programs and processes* (such as curriculum, instructional methods, class size, and grouping), and *outcomes* (such as student performance, dropout rates, employment, and further education)."

6. *Teachers should be involved in designing and using the assessment system.*

   "For an assessment system to help improve learning outcomes, teachers must fully understand its purposes and procedures and must be committed to, and use, the standards on which it is based. Therefore teachers should participate in the design, administration, scoring and use of assessment tasks and exercises."

7. *Assessment procedures and results should be understandable.*

   "Assessment information should be in a form that is useful to those who need it—students, teachers, parents, legislators, employers, postsecondary institutions, and the general public."

8. *The assessment system should be subject to continuous review and improvement.*

   "Large-scale, complex systems are rarely perfect, and even well-designed systems must be modified to adapt to changing conditions. Plans for the assessment system should provide for a continuing review process in which all concerned participate."

The National Forum on Assessment's criteria represent a growing consensus on the standards by which assessment programs should be judged. By mid-1992 those standards had been endorsed by more than eighty advocacy groups, professional organizations, and schools and colleges across the United States.

One of our biggest mistakes is the order in which we design educational systems. First we set up an organizational structure; then we plan the curriculum to fit the structure; and finally we decide criteria for student success. Not until this last step do we articulate the system's ultimate education purpose. . . . Given this process, it's not surprising that schooling seems so dysfunctional.

Fred M. Newmann,
Director of the National
Center on Effective
Secondary Schools,
University of Wisconsin-
Madison[9]

As the Forum freely admits, designing and implementing assessment programs that meet its criteria will not cure all the ills plaguing our education system. But without sound assessment programs, we cannot hope to diagnose those ills accurately or to evaluate the efficacy of proposed cures. That should be reason enough to make assessment programs that define standards and measure achievement accurately and fairly the starting point in our efforts to reform and restructure our schools.

Often-asked Questions About Authentic Assessment

Any discussion about new ways to evaluate students and schools quickly generates a host of questions and concerns. The most–asked questions focus on the expense and time involved in a change to more authentic forms of assessment. Other often-asked questions concern the objectivity, reliability, fairness, and the use of new assessment techniques.

Won't authentic assessment cost too much, especially compared to standardized tests?

The answer to this question depends on what costs are being compared. Standardized tests entail a tremendous expense in the development of individual test items, but are relatively inexpensive to administer and score on a per-student basis. Authentic assessment may prove less costly to develop but two to three times more expensive to administer and score. Those costs should drop as test banks accumulate and educators become more experienced and efficient at scoring the new assessments. The hope, of course, is that the costs of moving to authentic assessment will be largely offset by gains in teacher professionalism, improved instruction, and rising levels of student achievement.

> What we don't have is good cost-benefit evaluations of what's going on in testing across the country. One of the reasons is that nobody wants to fund that kind of research.
>
> *George Madaus,*
> *Director of the Center for the Study of Testing, Evaluation, and Educational Policy*[1]

Are assessments scored by people as reliable as machine-scored standardized tests?

No test gives perfectly reliable results, regardless of how it is scored. The SATs, for example, have a 40-point margin of error. Human evaluators, however, have been used successfully to judge competitions in sports, music, and art. Several states have used trained readers to score writing assessments and professional certification exams. Reliability can be maintained by the use of multiple judges, sound training procedures, clear scoring criteria, and ongoing checks of scoring consistency.

Can assessments scored by people be as objective as machine-scored tests?

Bias is a sticky issue in testing. Test companies promote machine scoring as a means of ensuring objective results. This assurance, however, does not address the question of whether the tests themselves are bias-free in their design.

Authentic assessment advocates answer concerns about objectivity in two ways. First, they promote open assessments that are available for scrutiny by anyone concerned about bias. Second, they maintain that judging bias can be minimized by scoring student work blind, by training evaluators to use scoring rubrics, by using group grading to promote scoring objectivity, and by auditing the scoring process to verify objectivity.

> An assessment in which you don't know either the task or the standards against which you will be judged is not only unfair, it's downright foolish if our aim is to get people good at important tasks.
>
> **Grant Wiggins,**
> *Executive Director of Consultants on Learning Assessment and School Structure*[2]

Is authentic assessment fair to all students?

Fairness is another tricky issue in assessment. Advocates of authentic assessment argue that the new assessments address the fairness issue in two ways. First, students know in advance what they will be asked to do and how they will be judged. This is inherently more fair to students than a secure test. Second, the flexibility of the new assessments promotes fairness by allowing teachers to accommodate individual differences in work pace, interests, learning style, and language proficiency.

Do students from diverse backgrounds score higher on authentic assessment tasks than on standardized tests?

Many teachers have embraced authentic assessment in the belief that it will yield a more accurate picture than standardized tests of what their students know and can do. While this may be true, it does not mean that test scores for all students will rise dramatically any time soon.

A study by the Center for Research on Evaluation, Standards, and Student Testing (CRESST) suggests that the performance gap between our least and most advantaged students is even greater on open-ended tasks than on standard multiple-choice tests. The reason, says CRESST, is that less advantaged children spend far more time being drilled in basic skills than being exposed to rich ideas and problem-solving activities. Clearly, changing assessment by itself cannot close this performance gap.

What special difficulties do students face when making the shift to authentic assessment?

Many teachers have found that students do not perform up to expectations when first confronted with open-ended assessments that call for higher-order thinking. The main reason seems to be that students conditioned by multiple-choice testing have not learned how to respond to questions that ask them to compare, explain, evaluate, or predict. The lesson these teachers have learned from early disappointments with authentic assessment is this: New forms of assessment should not be implemented without first evaluating students' proficiency in dealing with the kinds of questions, problems, and tasks that will be used and then using the results to fill in any gaps.

If instruction is defined primarily as "teacher talk," then alternative forms of evaluation are unquestionably intrusive and time-consuming because they have little to do with what is going on in the classroom. Teachers can't evaluate and lecture simultaneously.

Elizabeth Badger,
Director of Assessment,
Massachusetts
Department of Education[3]

How will students who are raised on authentic assessment perform on standardized tests?

The new assessments have not been around long enough to answer this question with any certainty. Generally students who perform well on authentic assessment tasks score well on standardized tests and vice versa.

This concern may fade away in time as standardized tests change to reflect new approaches to assessment. Such a change has already occurred in writing assessment. In the early 1980s, most states relied on standardized multiple-choice tests to assess writing skills. Today many states are using "standardized" performance tests to assess writing skills on a large scale.

Do authentic assessment tasks focus too much on process and skills at the expense of content knowledge?

In a well-designed assessment task, skills and content are inseparable. Content knowledge can be woven into a task in two ways. First, the task itself can be designed to focus on issues unique to a specific content area. Second, criteria dealing with content objectives can be made part of the scoring rubric.

Will the new assessments be more time-consuming for teachers than standardized tests?

Authentic assessment tasks often take longer to administer and score than standardized tests. If the tasks are well designed, however, the time spent by students should be virtually indistinguishable from time spent on other worthwhile learning activities. The time burden can be reduced by being selective about what to score, by making greater use of peer- and self-assessment, by integrating assessment into the classroom routine, and by having students do as much of the record keeping as possible.

How can teachers manage their classroom while taking time to assess just one or a few students?

Classroom management is a concern for most teachers when they begin using assessment techniques that divert their attention away from the entire class. One way to minimize problems is by providing engaging activities for the rest of the class while the teacher observes or interviews selected students. Another approach is to limit individual assessment to times when aides or volunteers are available to help monitor the class.

Classroom management is less of a problem for teachers who run a student-centered classroom. Students in such classrooms are trained to work independently, in groups or by themselves, for significant amounts of time, leaving the teacher free to make observations, conduct interviews, review portfolios, and so on without constant distractions.

What effect has authentic assessment had on changing instruction?

Authentic assessment has not been in place long enough to answer this question with any assurance. We do, however, have suggestive evidence from California that changing assessment can change instruction.

During the 1980s California abandoned its multiple-choice testing of writing skills in favor of assessments that had students produce a piece of writing in a specific genre. When asked about the impact of the new assessment approach, ninety-four percent of the teachers questioned said they were assigning a greater variety of writing tasks than in the past, while seventy-eight percent said they were also having students do more writing than before the change.

Rising test scores are no longer matters for public celebration because they are not matched by widespread demonstrations of real competence. Test scores in New York City, for instance, have been rising for a decade, and averages are now above national norms. But the popular view is that the city's schools are in a state of collapse, offering students too little substantial education.

Vito Perrone,
Director of
Teacher Education,
Harvard University[5]

Will the public accept authentic assessment?

We don't know. There is, however, a growing recognition that rising scores on standardized tests don't necessary mean that students are better educated than in the past. This disenchantment with traditional testing may help authentic assessment gain public support.

Is the change to authentic assessment worth the effort?

Too little is known about the quality, effects, and outcomes of authentic assessment to answer this question with any certainty. In time, enterprising educational researchers will surely fill this void with useful data. Until that happens, we have only the reports of those who have undertaken this change to rely on. Most of them would probably answer yes. But they would probably also add the caution not to underestimate the effort involved in successfully implementing a new assessment system.

The final and perhaps most unanswerable question at this point is whether authentic assessment represents a significant educational reform or whether, after an initial flurry of enthusiasm, it will become another short-lived educational fad. The answer will surely depend in part on the quality and results of early efforts to implement authentic assessment programs. It will probably depend also on how well educators communicate the purpose of new assessments to teachers, students, their families, and the community. Finally, it will depend on what our society values in education and is therefore willing to encourage and support.

Where to Find More Information

For those interested in learning more about authentic assessment, there are a number of places to turn to for information and ideas. You might begin by checking with your district and state assessment offices for an update on local and state initiatives. Look for presentations and workshops on assessment at local professional meetings and conferences. And if possible, spend some time at your nearest education library where you will find a number of books and articles on assessment. The titles listed below will help get you started.

Books

The new thinking on assessment has generated a flurry of books. Those listed here cover the practical whys, whats, and hows of authentic assessment.

Alverno College Faculty, *Assessment at Alverno College* (Milwaukee, Wis.: Alverno Productions, 1985). This report of a highly developed assessment program for college students is available from Alverno College, 3401 S. 39th Street, Milwaukee, WI 53215-4020.

Doug A. Archbald and Fred M. Newmann, *Beyond Standardized Testing: Assessing Authentic Academic Achievement in the Secondary School* (Reston, Va.: National Association of Secondary School Principals, 1988).

Jill Bartoli and Morton Botel, *Reading/Learning Disability: An Ecological Approach* (New York: Teachers College Press, 1988). Part III of this book presents the authors' views on "An Ecological Way of Evaluating."

Cathy Grace and Elizabeth F. Shores, *The Portfolio and Its Use: Developing Developmentally Appropriate Assessment for Young Children* (Little Rock, Ark.: Southern Association on Children Under Six, 1991).

Dominic F. Gullo, *Developmentally Appropriate Teaching in Early Childhood: Curriculum, Implementation, Evaluation* (Washington, D.C.: National Education Association, 1991).

Bill Harp, ed., *Assessment and Evaluation in Whole Language Programs* (Norwood, Mass.: Christopher-Gordon Publishers, Inc., 1991).

Joan L. Herman and Lynn Winters, *Tracking Your School's Success: A Guide to Sensible Evaluation* (Newbury Park, Ca.: Corwin Press, 1992).

Donald L. Hymes, Ann E. Chafin, and Peggy Gondor, *The Changing Face of Testing and Assessment: Problems and Solutions* (Arlington, Va.: American Association of School Administrators, 1991).

Gerald Kulm, ed., *Assessing Higher Order Thinking in Mathematics* (Washington, D.C.: American Association for the Advancement of Science, 1990).

Ruth Mitchell, *Testing for Learning: How New Approaches to Evaluation Can Improve American Schools* (New York: The Free Press, 1992).

Joseph D. Novak and D. Bob Gowin, *Learning How to Learn* (Cambridge University Press, 1984). A comprehensive and readable book on concept maps.

Karen L. Ostlund, *Science Process Skills: Assessing Hands-on Student Performance* (Menlo Park, Ca.: Addison-Wesley Publishing Company, 1992). Hands-on activities to assess students in grades 1 through 6.

Tej Pandey, the Mathematics Assessment Development Team, and the Mathematics Assessment Advisory Committee, *A Sampler of Mathematics Assessment* (Sacramento, Ca.: California Department of Education, 1991).

Walter C. Parker, *Renewing the Social Studies Curriculum* (Alexandria, Va.: Association for Supervision and Curriculum Development, 1991). The last chapter considers the place of authentic assessment in the social studies curriculum.

Vito Perrone, ed. *Expanding Student Assessment* (Alexandria, Va.: Association for Supervision and Curriculum Development, 1991). A collection of essays on many facets of assessment.

Thomas A. Romberg, ed., *Mathematics Assessment and Evaluation: Imperatives for Mathematics Educators* (Albany, N.Y.: State University of New York Press, 1992).

Jean Kerr Stenmark, ed., *Mathematics Assessment: Myths, Models, Good Questions, and Practical Suggestions* (Reston, Va.: National Council of Teachers of Mathematics, Inc., 1991).

Jean Kerr Stenmark and the EQUALS staff of the Assessment Committee of the California Mathematics Council Campaign for Mathematics, *Assessment Alternatives in Mathematics: An Overview of Assessment Techniques that Promote Learning* (Berkeley, Ca.: Lawrence Hall of Science, University of California, 1989).

Richard J. Stiggins, *Evaluating Students by Classroom Observation: Watching Students Grow* (Washington, D.C.: National Education Association, 1984). An early "how to" book on the design, use, and scoring of performance assessments.

Robert J. Tierney, Mark A. Carter, and Laura E. Desai, *Portfolio Assessment in the Reading-Writing Classroom* (Norwood, Mass.: Christopher-Gordon Publishers, Inc., 1991). A practical primer for teachers implementing portfolio assessment in language arts programs.

Journals

Articles on one aspect or another of the authentic assessment movement appear regularly in education journals and newsletters. A few journals have even devoted special issues to assessment. They include the following:

Arithmetic Teacher, February 1992. Look for several articles on the use of alternative assessments in math programs. Write: National Council of Teachers of Mathematics, 1906 Association Drive, Reston, VA 22091.

Educational Leadership, April 1989, February 1991, and May 1992. All three issues feature wide-ranging articles on the rationale and implementation of authentic assessment. Write: Association for Supervision and Curriculum Development, 125 N. West Street, Alexandria, VA 22314.

Horace, March 1990. This issue focuses on the subject of performance assessment. Write: The Coalition of Essential Schools, Box 1938, Brown University, Providence, RI 02912.

Language Arts, March 1990 and December 1991. The articles in the first issue all relate to evaluation of language and learning and in the second to literacy evaluation. Write: National Council of English Teachers, 1111 Kenyon Road, Urbana, IL 61801.

Phi Delta Kappan, May 1989. This issue examines testing and assessment from several points of view. Write: *Phi Delta Kappan,* P.O. Box 789, Bloomington, IN 47402.

Preventing School Failure, Winter 1992. The focus of this issue is "implementing curriculum-based measurement in the schools." Write: Helen Dwight Reid Education Foundation, 1319 Eighteenth Street, NW, Washington, DC 20036-1802.

Science Scope, March 1992. This issue is filled with practical articles on how to implement authentic assessment in science classrooms. Write: National Science Teachers Association, 1742 Connecticut Ave., NW, Washington, DC 20009.

Social Education, February 1992. See the special section on "student assessment in the social studies." Write: National Council for the Social Studies, 3501 Newark Street, NW, Washington, DC 20016.

Thrust for Educational Leadership, October 1991. This issue is aimed at administrators who are "developing and implementing new forms of student assessment." Write: Association of California School Administrators, 1575 Old Bayshore Highway, Burlingame, CA 94010.

Other Resources

A number of research projects, policy groups, coalitions, and networks have coalesced around the growing interest in assessment reform. The three listed below are representative of this trend.

The *National Forum on Assessment* is a coalition of education, civil rights, and advocacy organizations and institutions that have united to promote national "Criteria for Evaluation of Student Assessment Systems." For a more information about the criteria or to add your name or organization to the Forum's growing list of endorsements, contact the

National Forum on Assessment
c/o Council of Basic Education
725 15th Street, NW
Washington, DC 20005
(202) 347-4171

The *New Standards Project* is a large-scale, grass-roots effort to define challenging academic standards and to create assessments that reflect those standards. Funded by private foundations, the New Standards Project has already become a force in shaping policy makers' thinking on national student achievement standards and assessments. For more information contact either of the two directors of this project:

Learning Research and Development Center
3939 O'Hara Street, Room 408
Pittsburgh, PA 15260
(412) 624-8319

National Center on Education and the Economy
39 State Street, Suite 500
Rochester, NY 14614
(716) 546-7620

The *Portfolio Assessment Clearing House* is a network of educators involved in portfolio assessment. The Clearing House publishes a quarterly journal, *Portfolio News,* that provides members with descriptions of portfolio projects, discussions of general issues of concern in portfolio assessment, and an information exchange. To join the network write to the

Portfolio Assessment Clearing House
c/o San Dieguito Union High School District
710 Encinitas Boulevard
Encinitas, CA 92024

An Assessment Glossary

Accountability. The extent to which one is held responsible for one's actions or performance. In education, this has come to mean the demand that schools account for money spent on education by providing evidence of student learning and achievement.

Achievement test. A test designed to measure students' "school taught" learning in such areas as reading, writing, mathematics, and science.

Alternative assessment. A range of assessment methods designed to take the place of or to supplement standardized tests.

Analytic scoring. The awarding of separate scores for different traits or dimensions of a student's work. *See also* Primary trait scoring.

Anecdotal evidence. A narrative description of a child's behavior in a specific situation.

Assessment. The process of gathering and organizing data— often quantitative in nature and based on testing—to fulfill a variety of evaluation needs.

Audit. Rechecking assessment content and scoring to assure that the desired assessment standards have been met.

Authentic assessment. Assessment that both mirrors and measures students' performance in "real-life" tasks and situations. For example, if we want students to communicate effectively in writing, the authentic way to assess them is to evaluate actual samples of their writing.

Benchmark. A performance sample that serves as a standard against which other samples may be judged.

Blind scoring. The practice of minimizing bias by having evaluators score assessment products without knowing who produced them.

Calibration. Procedures for monitoring and adjusting scores of different evaluators to make them comparable. *See also* Group grading and moderation.

Checklist. A form used to keep track of a student's work or progress.

Competency test. An assessment designed to make sure that students have met minimal content and skill standards. Generally students are required to pass such tests as a condition of promotion or graduation.

Concept mapping. An assessment technique based on clustering that is used to determine how well students understand concepts and relationships between concepts.

Conference recording form. *See* Interview sheet.

Content standards. The knowledge, skills, and understandings schools should teach for students to attain high levels of competency in challenging subject areas.

Criterion-referenced test. An assessment designed to reveal what a student knows, understands, or can do in relation to specific objectives. Criterion-referenced tests are intended to identify strengths and weaknesses in individual students in terms of knowledge or skills.

Culturally relevant assessment. Assessment that addresses the unique cultural aspects of class, school, and community among diverse populations.

Curriculum alignment. The process of matching curriculum to the scope and sequence of a testing program to ensure that teachers will cover the material on the test.

Curriculum-embedded assessment. Assessment used as part of the regular instructional program and at a time deemed most appropriate by the teacher. Embedded assessments generally require students to pull together and apply what they know in an informal classroom setting rather than in a formal test situation.

Descriptors. A set of clearly specified signs or criteria for determining a student's level of achievement on an assessment task. Descriptors tell the evaluator what to look for and then how to place that work on a predetermined scale. Example: "The student describes the problem adequately and argues convincingly for at least one solution."

Developmental checklist. A listing of the traits or behaviors a teacher should be watching for while observing students.

Dimensions. The traits or features to be used in judging a student's performance or product. In a writing assessment, the important dimensions might include coherence, tone, and correctness of grammar. *See also* Traits.

Embedded assessment. *See* Curriculum-embedded assessment.

Enhanced multiple-choice question. A multiple-choice question that has been enhanced, or improved, to make it more than a passive-recall test item. Such questions may ask students to interpret a primary source, to classify works of art, to draw inferences from a map, or to justify their choice in a short written response.

Essay question. An assessment task that calls for a structured, written response.

Evaluation. The process of interpreting or making judgments about assessment data to determine the extent to which students are achieving instructional objectives.

Event task. A performance task designed to assess complex skills or competencies that may take one or more class periods to complete.

Exhibition. The production of discourse, things, or performances for a public. Generally, exhibitions require the integration of a broad range of competencies and considerable student initiative and responsibility in carrying them out.

Exhibition of mastery. A performance of important understandings and abilities to demonstrate that the student has achieved a high level of competence.

Experienced curriculum. Those things that a student chooses to emphasize, elaborate on, ignore, or omit in his or her personal "curriculum of the mind" as opposed to the formal or taught curriculum.

Extended task. A performance task, designed to assess broad competencies, that may take weeks or months to complete.

External evaluation. Evaluation by people other than the classroom teacher.

Free-response question. Assessment tasks that encourage varied responses such as written explanations, drawings, and diagrams. *See also* Open-ended question.

Fishbowl format. A small group discussion format in which the participants gather in the center of the room while the remaining students and teacher observe from a larger, outer circle.

Group grading. A technique for increasing the objectivity and reliability of scoring of large-scale assessments by people as opposed to machines. *See also* Calibration.

High-stakes assessment. Testing that has strong consequences for the participants. For teachers such consequences might include hiring or promotion decisions. For students performance might affect entry into a special class, college admission, or the awarding of a diploma or degree. The SAT is an example of a high-stakes test.

Holistic assessment. *See* Authentic assessment.

Holistic scoring. Scoring based on an overall impression of a work rather than on an accumulation of points.

Interview sheet. A form used to guide student interviews and conferences. Generally the interview sheet consists of a list of questions to be asked by the teacher with space for recording the student's responses.

Journal. An ongoing, written record of a student's thoughts on self-selected topics of personal interest. A *personal journal* is usually private unless the student invites a teacher or classmate to read an entry. A *dialogue journal* is an extended written interchange between a teacher or other specialist and a student on a topic of mutual interest. Journal writing gives students practice in writing while encouraging the habit of reflective thinking.

Learning log. An ongoing record of students' accomplishments and future goals. Like journals, learning logs can be used to encourage self-assessment and metacognition.

Low-stakes assessment. Testing that has few direct consequences for the participants. Such testing is generally used for diagnosis of individual students or to provide information for such purposes as instructional improvement or curriculum redesign.

Moderation. The process of collectively establishing and maintaining shared scoring standards across many evaluators. Moderation may be done informally by teachers who exchange a few scored papers with other teachers for evaluation to check that their standards are the same, or it may done more formally in a group grading session.

Norm. The midpoint in the distribution of scores obtained in testing a large group of students. By definition, fifty percent of tested students score above the norm, and fifty percent score below.

Norm-referenced test. A standardized assessment designed to place a student or group of students in rank order compared to other test takers of the same age and grade.

Objectivity. The measure of whether a test is free from bias or subjectivity in design and scoring.

Observations. The sort of information that teachers note in their everyday work with students. Observation data may be recorded in rating forms, checklists, student profiles, narrative descriptions, and anecdotal records.

On-demand assessment. Testing at a predetermined time and place with little or no teacher or student discretion.

Open-ended task. A performance task in which students are given a stimulus or prompt and then asked to communicate a response. Tasks may be more or less open depending on how many restrictions or directions are included.

Outcome-based assessment. Assessment that is designed to "test to the objectives." Instead of emphasizing what a student has not mastered, outcome-based assessment generally emphasizes what a student has learned.

Outcome-based education. Education that is focused on clearly and publicly stated objectives and outcomes. Ideally the stated curriculum is the taught curriculum and the taught curriculum is the tested curriculum.

Perform.   To carry out or bring to completion. In the assessment context, performing should involve displaying one's "knowledge in use."

Performance assessment.   Direct, systematic observation and assessment based on student performances or performance samples and established performance criteria.

Performance samples.   Tangible documents or artifacts that carry the stamp of student accomplishments.

Performance standards.   The quality of student performance required to demonstrate various levels of competency in each subject area.

Performance tasks.   Tasks given to students to assess their ability to achieve desired outcomes. Such tasks may vary from short test-like items to complex projects that extend over a considerable length of time. Performance tasks may be more or less "authentic" insofar as they simulate real-life challenges and problems.

Portfolio.   A file, folder, computer disk, or box containing information and work samples that document a student's growth and accomplishments over time.

Primary trait scoring.   The awarding of separate scores for the primary, or most important, dimensions of a student's work. In writing assessment, primary trait scoring looks first for the expected features of the specific genre.

Process.   A series of linked actions and behaviors that together lead toward a desired result such as clear communication or effective teamwork.

Process assessment.   Assessment that focuses on how well students have mastered an entire process or set of inter-related skills.

Product. The concrete outcome of student effort. A student product may be written, drawn, constructed, taped, or otherwise recorded for evaluation.

Profile. A form filled out by a teacher, student, or family member that provides information about a student's interests, traits, abilities, achievements, and so on.

Prompt. A description of a topic, situation, or scenario to which students are expected to respond in some way.

Rank ordering. The listing of scores or ratings in order from the highest to lowest or vice versa.

Rater. An evaluator trained to rate or score tests, portfolios, performance tasks, or other assessments according to specific scoring criteria.

Rating. A judgment made about the relative position of a student's ability or performance. In authentic assessment, this judgment is often guided by a scoring rubric.

Reliability. A measure of the constancy of scoring outcomes over time or over many evaluators. A test is considered reliable if the same answers produce the same score no matter when and how the scoring is done.

Rubric. An established set of criteria for scoring or rating students' tests, portfolios, or performances.

Sampling. A way to get information about a large group by examining only a small number of the group, the sample. *Student sampling* involves the identification of a subset of students to test whose performance will accurately represent the entire student population. *Curriculum sampling* involves the selection of a small number of test items to represent the entire curriculum. *Matrix sampling* does both at once by giving different student samples different curriculum samples.

Scaffolding.   Information included in test questions or assessment tasks to help focus students' attention on what to include in their responses.

Scale.   The range of scores possible for a test or assessment. Authentic assessments typically use a 4- to 6-point scale, compared to a scale of 100 or more for standardized tests.

Scored discussion.   A small group discussion on a specified topic in which the participants are awarded points for positive contributions, such as asking a clarifying question, and lose points for negative behaviors, such as monopolizing the conversation.

Secure.   Secret or unavailable for previewing. A test is secure when students and teachers do not have prior access to it to help them prepare. In contrast to traditional testing, authentic assessment emphasizes open or nonsecure tests. Students and teachers often know in advance what they will be asked to do and are encouraged to prepare accordingly.

Specification.   The public description of performance standards for an assessment. A detailed specification would describe the performance task, the content involved, the cognitive demands of the activity, and scoring criteria.

Stakeholder.   Anyone who has an interest, or stake, in an assessment.

Standard.   In assessment, a standard is a level of performance established by the testing authority to differentiate scores obtained by students. Standards add meaning to scores by determining the level at which students pass, fail, or excel. In curriculum development, standards define a level a achievement toward which all students should strive.

Standardized tests.   Mass-produced, machine-scored tests designed to measure skills and knowledge that are assumed to be taught in a reasonably standardized way.

Stimulus. The focal point of a question or assessment task. Possible stimuli include problems, scenarios, cartoons, maps, primary sources, diagrams, paintings, and graphs.

Systemic validity. A measure of how well a test induces changes in the education system that foster the development of the competencies the test is designed to assess.

Task. A goal-directed assessment activity. An authentic assessment task demands that students bring a broad range of knowledge and skills to bear on a complex problem.

Test. A measuring instrument for assessing and documenting student learning. The traditional test is a single-occasion, one-dimensional, timed exercise.

Testing. An assessment method specifically designed to measure and document student learning.

Traits. The dimensions or features to be used in judging a student's performance or product. In a mathematics assessment, the relevant traits might include use of a calculator and the accuracy of calculations. *See also* Dimensions.

Validity. A measure of how well an assessment relates to what students are expected to have learned. A valid assessment measures what it is supposed to measure and not some peripheral features.

Verification. The process of assuring that the desired assessment standards have been met.

Writing prompt. A description of a topic, scenario, or situation to which students are expected to respond in writing. Well-crafted writing prompts also include information on the purpose of and audience for the student's response.

Notes and Credits

Introduction

1. Kathleen B. Comfort, "Crime Solvers in California," *Science Scope* (Mar. 1992), p. 56. Reprinted with permission from National Science Teachers Association Publications.

Chapter One

1. Larry Malone, "Assessment and Elementary School Science," *Science Assessment Colloquium*, Arizona Department of Education, Feb. 24, 1992.

2. This story is told in the book of Judges, chapter 12.

3. Robert B. Reich, *The Work of Nations* (New York: Alfred A. Knopf, 1991), pp. 59–60.

4. Ron Brandt, "On Misuse of Testing: A Conversation with George Madaus," *Educational Leadership*, Apr. 1989, p. 27.

5. Walter Haney and George Madaus, "Searching for Alternatives to Standardized Tests: Whys, Whats, and Whithers," *Phi Delta Kappan*, May 1989, p. 684.

6. From Ruth Mitchell, *Testing for Learning: How New Approaches to Evaluation Can Improve American Schools* (New York: The Free Press, 1992), p. 16. Reprinted by permission of Macmillan Publishing Co.

Chapter Two

1. Grant Wiggins, "A True Test: Toward More Authentic and Equitable Assessment," *Phi Delta Kappan*, May 1989, pp. 703–4.

2. Ibid. p. 711.

3. Grant Wiggins, "Teaching to the (Authentic) Test," *Educational Leadership*, Vol. 46 (Apr. 1989), p. 45. Reprinted with permission of the Association for Supervision and Curriculum Development. Copyright 1989 by ASCD. All rights reserved.

4. From Pat Nickell, "'Doing the Stuff of Social Studies': A Conversation with Grant Wiggins," *Social Education*, Feb. 1992, p. 94. Copyright by the National Council for the Social Studies. Reprinted by permission.

5. From *Expanding Student Assessment*, Vito Perrone, ed. (Alexandria, Va.: Association for Supervision and Curriculum Development, 1991), p. 62. Reprinted with permission of the Association for Supervision and Curriculum Development. All rights reserved.

6. From Doug A. Archbald and Fred M. Newmann, *Beyond Standardized Testing: Assessing Authentic Academic Achievement in the Secondary School* (Reston, Va.: National Association of Secondary School Principles, 1988), p. 3. Reprinted by permission.

7. *Expanding Student Assessment*, p. 116.

Chapter Three

1. Jill Bartoli and Morton Botel, *Reading/Learning Disability: An Ecological Approach* (New York: Teachers College Press, 1988), p. 190.

2. Adapted from *The Block Book*, rev. ed., Elisabeth S. Hirsch, ed. (National Association for the Education of Young Children, Washington, D.C., 20009, 1984), pp. 103–109.

3. From *Assessment and Evaluation in Whole Language Programs*, Bill Harp, ed. (Norwood, Mass.: Christopher-Gordon Publishers, Inc., 1991), p. 79. Used with permission of the publisher.

4. From Ruth Mitchell, *Testing for Learning: How New Approaches to Evaluation Can Improve American Schools* (New York: The Free Press, 1992), p. 152. Reprinted by permission of Macmillan Publishing Co.

5. Adrienne L. Herrell, Ph.D., "Assessment in Early Childhood Programs," (California State University, Fresno, June 1990), p. 49, figs. 3.3, 3.4.

6. Harp, p. 39.

7. Mitchell, p. 150.

8. Mitchell, p. 139. This form was developed by the Center for Language in Primary Education, Inner London Education Authority (1988, 1989).

Chapter Four

1. From Jane Hansen, "Literacy Portfolios: Helping Students Know Themselves," *Educational Leadership*, Vol. 49 (May 1992), p. 66. Reprinted with permission of the Association for Supervision and Curriculum Development. Copyright 1992 by ASCD.

2. John I. Goodlad, *A Place Called School: Prospects for the Future* (New York: McGraw-Hill Book Co., 1984), p. 15.

3. Hansen, p. 68.

4. Linda Vavrus, "Put Portfolios to the Test," *Instructor*, August 1990, p. 53.

5. Darlene M. Frazier and F. Leon Paulson, "How Portfolios Motivate Reluctant Writers," *Educational Leadership*, May 1992, p. 64.

6. From "A Conversation with Grant Wiggins," *Instructor*, Aug. 1990, p. 51.

7. From Dennie Palmer Wolf, "Portfolio Assessment: Sampling Student Work," *Educational Leadership*, Vol. 46 (Apr. 1989), pp. 36–38. Reprinted with permission of the Association for Supervision and Curriculum Development. Copyright 1989 by ASCD.

8. Scott Willis, "'Quality by Design' Through Portfolios," *ASCD Update*, June 1992, p. 2.

9. Margie Krest, "Adapting the Portfolio to Meet Student Needs," *English Journal*, Feb. 1990, p. 30.

10. Jay Simmons, "Portfolios as Large-scale Assessment," *Language Arts*, Mar. 1990, pp. 262–67.

11. Elizabeth A. Hebert, "Portfolios Invite Reflection—from Students *and* Staff," *Educational Leadership*, May 1992, pp. 58–61.

12. "Writing Evaluation: Picture of a Portfolio," *Instructor*, Mar. 1992, p. 29.

13. John B. Thomas, "The New Report Cards," *Better Homes and Gardens*, May 1991, p. 36.

14. "Writing Evaluation," p. 29.

15. From Pam Knight, "How I Use Portfolios in Mathematics," *Educational Leadership*, Vol. 49 (May 1992), pp. 71–72. Reprinted with permission of the Association for Supervision and Curriculum Development. Copyright 1992 by ASCD.

16. Ibid. p. 72.

17. From Paul Stemmer, Bill Brown, and Catherine Smith, "The Employability Skills Portfolio," *Educational Leadership*, Vol. 49 (May 1992), p. 33. Reprinted with permission of the Association for Supervision and Curriculum Development. Copyright 1992 by ASCD.

18. Wolf, pp. 35–39.

19. Wolf, p. 37.

20. Farai Chideya, "Surely for the Spirit, But Also for the Mind," *Newsweek*, Dec. 2, 1991, p. 61.

21. From Jo Campbell, "Laser Disk Portfolios: Total Child Assessment," *Educational Leadership*, May 1992, pp. 69–70.

22. Ibid. p. 70.

23. From *Expanding Student Assessment*, Vito Perrone, ed. (Alexandria, Va.: Association for Supervision and Curriculum Development, 1991), pp. 38–39. Reprinted with permission of the Association for Supervision and Curriculum Development. All rights reserved.

Chapter Five

1. From Mathematics Assessment: *Myths, Models, Good Questions, and Practical Suggestions,* Jean Kerr Stenmark, ed., University of California (Reston, Va.: National Council of Teachers of Mathematics, 1991), p. 12.

2. Grant Wiggins, "Teaching to the (Authentic) Test," *Educational Leadership*, Vol. 46 (Apr. 1989), p. 41. Reprinted with permission of the Association for Supervision and Curriculum Development. Copyright 1989 by ASCD. All rights reserved.

3. From Grant Wiggins, "Creating Tests Worth Taking," *Educational Leadership*, May 1992, p. 26. Copyright by Grant Wiggins.

4. Lorrie A. Shepard, "Why We Need Better Assessments," *Educational Leadership*, Apr. 1989, p. 6.

5. Kentucky Department of Education. Reprinted with permission.

6. Wiggins, "Creating," pp. 26–27.

7. From Elizabeth Badger, "More Than Testing," *Arithmetic Teacher*, May 1992, p. 9. Copyright 1992 by the National Council of Teachers of Mathematics.

8. From Benjamin S. Bloom, "The Search for Methods of Group Instruction as Effective as One-on-One Tutoring," *Educational Leadership*, May 1984, p. 14. Copyright by Benjamin S. Bloom.

9. From Elementary Science Example from *Learning by Doing: A Manual for Teaching and Assessing Higher Order Thinking in Science and Mathematics.* National Assessment of Educational Progress.

10. From the 1991 CAP field test collection: "Working Materials." Reprinted by permission of the California Assessment Program, California Department of Education.

11. From *A Sampler of Authentic Assessment,* prepared by Dr. Ruth Mitchell for Beyond the Bubble, 1989 Curriculum/Assessment Alignment Conferences, Sacramento and Long Beach, Calif.

12. Reprinted by permission from *A Sampler of Mathematics Assessment* (California Department of Education, P.O. Box 271, Sacramento, Calif. 95812-0271, 1991), p. 52.

13. James Killoran, "In Defense of the Multiple-Choice Question," *Social Education*, Feb. 1992, p. 108.

14. Kentucky Department of Education. Reprinted with permission.

15. *California Assessment Program Secondary History-Social Science Sample Test Items,* Form H 1002. Reprinted by permission of the California Assessment Program, California Department of Education.

16. From Deborah J. Tippins and Nancy Fichtman Dana, "Culturally Relevant Alternative Assessment," *Science Scope,* Mar. 1992, p. 51.

17. From Ruth Mitchell, *Testing for Learning: How New Approaches to Evaluation Can Improve American Schools* (New York: The Free Press, 1992), pp. 47–49. Reprinted by permission of Macmillan Publishing Co.

18. From Doug A. Archbald and Fred M. Newmann, *Beyond Standardized Testing: Assessing Authentic Academic Achievement in the Secondary School* (Reston, Va.: National Association of Secondary School Principles, 1988), pp. 10–13. Reprinted by permission.

19. John Zola, "Scored Discussions," *Social Education,* Vol. 56 (Feb. 1992), pp. 123–25. Copyright by the National Council for the Social Studies. Reprinted by permission.

20. Zola, p. 125.

21. *Mathematics Assessment,* p. 15

22. From Coalition of Essential Schools newsletter *Horace,* Brown University, Education Dept., Providence, R.I.

23. From *Expanding Student Assessment,* Vito Perrone, ed. (Alexandria, Va.: Association for Supervision and Curriculum Development, 1991), pp. 106, 116. Reprinted with permission of the Association for Supervision and Curriculum Development. All rights reserved.

24. Shirley Lauterbach and V. Daniel Ochs, "Performance Assessment: Everyone Talks About It, But What Is It?" *NSTA Reports,* Dec. 1991/Jan. 1992, p. 10.

25. Wiggins, "Teaching," p. 43.

26. Ibid. p. 42.

27. From Rite of Passage Experience (R.O.P.E.) Student Handbook at Walden III Alternative Secondary School, Racine, Wis. Reprinted by permission.

28. Wiggins, "Teaching," p. 43.

29. Archbald and Newmann, pp. 17–18.

30. Dale Carlson, "Changing the Face of Testing in California," *California Curriculum News Report,* Jan.-Feb. 1991, p. 1.

Chapter Six

1. Donald Graves, *Writing: Teachers and Students at Work* (Exeter, N.H.: Heinemann Educational Books, 1983), p. 314.

2. David Dillon, *Language Arts,* Mar. 1990, p. 238.

3. Linda Leonard Lamme and Cecilia Hysmith, "One School's Adventure into Portfolio Assessment," *Language Arts,* Dec. 1991, p. 632.

4. Lamme and Hysmith, p. 634.

5. From *Mathematics Assessment: Myths, Models, Good Questions, and Practical Suggestions,* Jean Kerr Stenmark, ed., University of California (Reston, Va.: National Council of Teachers of Mathematics, 1991), p. 55.

6. Linda Rief, "Finding the Value in Evaluation: Self-assessment in a Middle School Classroom," *Educational Leadership,* Mar. 1990, p. 29

7. From *Toolbox,* British Colombia Ministry of Education (Victoria, B.C.: The Ministry).

8. Fig. 6.7 from Ch. 6, "A Collage of Assessment and Evaluation from Primary Classrooms," *Assessment and Evaluation in Whole Language Programs,* Bill Harp, ed., (Norwood, Mass.: Christopher-Gordon Publishers, Inc., 1991), p. 106. Used by permission of the publisher.

9. Linda Culp and Virginia Malone, "Peer Scores for Group Work," *Science Scope,* Mar. 1992, p. 36. Reprinted with permission from National Science Teachers Association Publications, 1742 Connecticut Ave., N.W., Washington, D.C. 20009-1171.

10. From *Expanding Student Assessment,* Vito Perrone, ed. (Alexandria, Va.: Association for Supervision and Curriculum Development, 1991), p. 37. Reprinted with permission of the Association for Supervision and Curriculum Development. All rights reserved.

11. From Ch. 11, "A Principal's View on Reporting Progress," *Assessment and Evaluation in Whole Language* Programs, Bill Harp, ed., (Norwood, Mass.: Christopher-Gordon Publishers, Inc., 1991), p. 214. Used by permission of the publisher.

12. From Ruth Mitchell, *Testing for Learning: How New Approaches to Evaluation Can Improve American Schools* (New York: The Free Press, 1992), p. 114. Reprinted by permission of Macmillan Publishing Co.

13. From Kathryn Howard, "Making the Writing Portfolio Real," *Quarterly of the National Writing Project and the Center for the Study of Writing,* Vol. 12 (Spring 1990), pp. 4–7, 27.

14. Mitchell, p. 89.

Chapter Seven

1. From an interview with Frank Huyette.

2. From Texas Elementary Inservice Project, 1991. Developed for the Texas Educational Agency, Title II, Project No. 00690401. Science Education Center, College of Education, University of Texas at Austin.

3. Gene I. Maeroff, "Assessing Alternative Assessment," *Phi Delta Kappan,* Dec. 1991, p. 278.

4. From "Elementary Mathematics Examples," *Benchmarks: Standards of Student Achievement* (Toronto Board of Education). Reprinted with permission of the Toronto Board of Education, Ontario.

5. From *Benchmarks, Vermont Portfolio Assessment* (Vermont Department of Education), No. 26.

6. California Assessment Program (CAP), *A Question of Thinking: A First Look at Students' Performance on Open-ended Questions in Mathematics* (Sacramento, Calif.: California State Department of Education, 1989).

7. From Krista Ramsey, School Smart Parents, "Writing Tests Help Teachers Evaluate Student Performance," *Cincinnati Enquirer,* 1990.

8. From *Analytic Assessment Guide,* Vermont Assessment Program.

9. Richard P. Mills, "Portfolios Capture Rich Array of Student Performance," *The School Administrator,* Dec. 1989, p. 11.

10. From *"This Is My Best": The Report of Vermont's Writing Assessment Program* (Vermont Department of Education, 1991), p. 13.

11. Robert J. Tierney, Mark A. Carter, and Laura E. Desai, *Portfolio Assessment in the Reading-Writing Classroom* (Norwood, Mass.: Christopher-Gordon Publishers, Inc., 1991), p. 15.

12. From Jane Hancock, "But . . . What About Grades," *Portfolio News,* Vol. 2 (Winter 1991), p. 3.

13. Margie Krest, "Adapting the Portfolio to Meet Student Needs," *English Journal,* Feb. 1990, p. 29.

14. Ibid. p. 30.
15. Ibid.
16. Ibid.
17. Ibid. pp. 31, 33.

Chapter Eight

1. Inez Fugate Liftig, Bob Liftig, and Karen Eaker, "Making Assessment Work: What Teachers Should Know Before They Try It," *Science Scope*, Mar. 1992, pp. 4–8.

2. From Ronald Brandt, "On Performance Assessment: A Conversation with Grant Wiggins," *Educational Leadership*, Vol. 40 (May 1992), p. 35. Reprinted with permission of the Association for Supervision and Curriculum Development. Copyright 1992 by ASCD. All rights reserved.

3. Donald J. Kemp and Winfield Cooper, "Teamwork with Teachers," *Thrust for Educational Leadership*, Oct. 1991, p. 29. Published by the Association of California School Administrators.

4. Ibid.

5. Janet L. McDaid and Donna G. Davis, "Using Assessment Results Wisely," *Thrust for Educational Leadership*, Oct. 1991, p. 35.

6. Theodore R. Sizer, *Horace's Compromise: The Dilemma of the American High School* (Boston: Houghton Mifflin Company, 1985), p. 228.

7. From National Forum on Assessment, Ruth Mitchell and Monty Neill, co-chairs, "Criteria for Evaluation of Student Assessment Systems" and "The Development and Use of the National Forum on Assessment's Criteria for Evaluation of Student Assessment Systems," 1991.

8. National Forum on Assessment, "Criteria for Evaluation."

9. Fred M. Newmann, "Linking Restructuring to Authentic Student Achievement," *Phi Delta Kappan*, Vol. 72 (Feb. 1991), p. 459. Copyright Feb. 1991, Phi Delta Kappan.

Chapter Nine

1. Ronald Brandt, "On Misuse of Testing: A Conversation with George Madaus," *Educational Leadership*, Vol. 46 (Apr. 1989), p. 28. Reprinted with permission of the Association for Supervision and Curriculum Development. Copyright 1989 by ASCD. All rights reserved.

2. From Pat Nickell, "'Doing the Stuff of Social Studies': A Conversation with Grant Wiggins," *Social Education*, Feb. 1992, p. 92. Copyright by the National Council for the Social Studies. Reprinted by permission.

3. From Elizabeth Badger, "More Than Testing," *Arithmetic Teacher*, May 1992, p. 10. Copyright 1992 by the National Council of Teachers of Mathematics.

4. *Report on Education Research*, September 18, 1991, p. 5.

5. From *Expanding Student Assessment*, Vito Perrone, ed. (Alexandria, Va.: Association for Supervision and Curriculum Development, 1991), p. vii. Reprinted with permission of the Association for Supervision and Curriculum Development. All rights reserved.